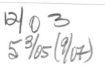

The Greatest Minds and Ideas of All Time

WILL DURANT

Compiled and edited by John Little

Simon & Schuster

NEW YORK   LONDON   TORONTO   SYDNEY   SINGAPORE

SIMON & SCHUSTER
Rockefeller Center
1230 Avenue of the Americas
New York, NY 10020

For information regarding special discounts for bulk purchases,
please contact Simon & Schuster Special Sales at
1-800-456-6798 or business@simonandschuster.com

DESIGNED BY PAUL DIPPOLITO

Manufactured in the United States of America

1 3 5 7 9 10 8 6 4 2

Library of Congress Cataloging-in-Publication Data

Durant, Will, date.
The greatest minds and ideas of all time / Will Durant ;
compiled and edited by John Little.
p. cm.
Includes index.
1. Civilization—History. 2. Intellectual life—History.
I. Little, John R., date. II. Title.

CB69 .D86 2002
909—dc21   2002075852

ISBN 0-7432-3553-3

If a man is fortunate he will, before he dies, gather up as much as he can of his civilized heritage and transmit it to his children. And to his final breath he will be grateful for this inexhaustible legacy, knowing that it is our nourishing mother and our lasting life.

—WILL DURANT

Keeping the above observation of Will Durant's in mind, I should dedicate this compendium of the peaks of our human heritage to all children, and more prejudicially, to my children: Riley, Taylor, Brandon, and Benjamin; that they may learn and experience the noble strain in humanity and learn that man is capable of such great things that even the gods might be envious.

And to Edward and Benny Easton, whose grandparents worked so hard through so many decades to deliver this gift to them.

—JOHN LITTLE

Contents

*The Greatest
Minds and Ideas
of All Time*

Introduction

In 1968, shortly after winning the Pulitzer Prize for literature, Will Durant and his wife, Ariel, consented to a television interview to be conducted in their home in Los Angeles, California. The interviewer, who fancied himself something of an intellectual, posed to Durant the following question:

> *If I were to ask you to name the person who has most influenced our century (the 20th century) would it be Karl Marx?*

Durant paused for a moment and then replied:

> *Well, if you use the word in its largest sense, we would have to give the greatest share of* influence *to the technical inventors, to men like Edison. Doubtless the development of electricity has transformed the world even more than any Marxian propaganda. Then, if you think in terms of ideas, I think the influence of Darwin is still greater than the influence of Marx, but in a different field. The basic phenomenon of our time is not Communism; it's the decline of religious belief, which has all sorts of effects on morals and even on politics because religion has been a tool of politics. But today in Europe it ceases to be a tool, it has very little influence in determining political decisions—whereas 500 years ago, the pope was superior in influence to any civil ruler on earth.*

Later, during the same interview, the interviewer turned to his subject and asked:

> *Dr. Durant, of all the characters populating* The Story of Civilization, *whom would you have most liked to have known?*

Durant contemplated the question seriously and then, poker-faced, replied, "Madame De Pompadour."

The interviewer was dumbfounded.

"Why is that?" he asked.

A twinkle came to Durant's eyes as he answered, "Well, she was beautiful, she was charming, she was luscious—what *else* do you want?"

I cite these two anecdotes not simply to reveal Durant's views on the influence of inventors and biologists on human history, nor even his tendency to use wit to disarm journalists who took themselves or their vocations too seriously (he once noted that humor is akin to philosophy for they are both viewpoints born of a large perspective of life), but rather to show that his opinion on assessing the significance of individuals and events from human history was something that was constantly sought after—sometimes twice in the same interview.

It is entirely understandable that Durant should find himself asked to answer such questions. Any time a man spends over half a century researching and writing an eleven-volume integral history of civilization, it is natural that people are going to want to know what conclusions he has drawn from the enterprise; to know what eras, individuals, and achievements stood out in his mind as being the greatest or most significant. Who, for example, would Durant rate on his Roll of Honor of human thought as the greatest thinkers in human history? Who would he rate as the truly great poets; the ones that plucked notes upon heartstrings that continue to resonate hundreds and thousands of years after their passing? And what would be the absolute best books one should read in order to receive a meaningful—and useful—education? Over the course of Durant's career, he responded to the increasing public demand for such qualified assessments by putting pen to paper and crafting a series of essays containing his personal ranking of "The Ten Greatest Thinkers," "The Ten Greatest Poets," "The One Hundred Best Books for an Education," "The Ten Peaks of Human Progress," and "Twelve Vital Dates in World History." Certain of these essays were published in periodicals; others were presented as lectures to standing-room-only attendees. However, unless you happened to purchase those magazines, or were fortunate enough to attend one of those lectures, it would not have been possible to learn of his conclusions in these matters. Fortunately, all of these essays have been brought together in *The Greatest Minds and Ideas of All Time*.

To formulate a ranking system and then apply it to such a broad array of human achievement is a difficult undertaking, to be sure, but Durant (as always) succeeds brilliantly; he not only presents compelling evidence for his selections, but also stimulates the reader to form his or her own opinions and to look beyond immediate surroundings and present culture and into a timeless realm, which he called "The Country of the Mind," a sort of cerebral retirement home wherein the heroes of our species dwell after having served their time and purpose in their respective eras and where to be human is something to be lauded. Indeed, the title of the first chapter of this book serves to frame its very thesis: "A Shameless Worship of Heroes."

The philosophy that resonates from the pages of all of Durant's books, but most particularly in *The Greatest Minds and Ideas of All Time,* is unabashedly "prohuman" and serves to underscore the splendor of our intellectual and artistic heritage. In fact, Durant was known as the "gentle philosopher" and the "radical saint," as he always sought to report on the positive achievements in human events and history. In a sentence, Durant chose to illuminate with his pen the mountain peaks of greatness in our species' history.

The Greatest Minds and Ideas of All Time is a book containing the absolute best of our heritage passed on for the edification and benefit of future generations, replete with Durant's renowned erudition, wit, and unique ability to explain the profoundest of events and ideas in simple and exciting terms. It is a book that serves both as a wonderful introduction to the writings of Will Durant and as a summing up, a quantification of genius, a travel guide to the "must-see" stops in the landscape of human history.

In many respects this book is a wonderful and logical companion volume to Durant's *Heroes of History*. Most notably, whereas *Heroes of History* is an overview of over one hundred centuries of human achievement, *The Greatest Minds and Ideas of All Time* provides Durant's personal assessment of it. Moreover, *The Greatest Minds and Ideas of All Time* contains profiles of three individuals (Darwin, Keats, and Whitman) that had been intended for inclusion in the *Heroes of History* book, but owing to a series of personal calamities, culminating in Durant's death in 1981, were omitted from the text (indeed, the intended final two chapters of *Heroes*—Durant's last book—would never be composed).

Through prose that rises at times to the heights of poetry, *The Greatest Minds and Ideas of All Time* is an extension of Durant's long-standing invitation to enter the world of the "best of the best," and a means by which one can come to recognize and befriend genius. The dividends from such an enterprise are many, for as Durant once noted:

> *We cannot live long in that celestial realm of all genius without becoming a little finer than we were. And though we shall not find there the poignant delirium of youth, we shall know a lasting, gentle happiness, a profound delight which time cannot take from us until it takes all.*

—John Little

CHAPTER ONE
A Shameless Worship of Heroes

OF THE MANY IDEALS which in youth gave life a meaning and radiance missing from the chilly perspectives of middle age, one at least has remained with me as bright and satisfying as ever before—the shameless worship of heroes. In an age that would level everything and reverence nothing, I take my stand with Victorian Carlyle, and light my candles, like Mirandola before Plato's image, at the shrines of great men.

I say *shameless,* for I know how unfashionable it is now to acknowledge in life or history any genius loftier than ourselves. Our democratic dogma has leveled not only all voters but all leaders; we delight to show that living geniuses are only mediocrities, and that dead ones are myths. If we may believe historian H. G. Wells, Caesar was a numbskull and Napoleon a fool. Since it is contrary to good manners to exalt ourselves, we achieve the same result by slyly indicating how inferior are the great men of the earth. In some of us, perhaps, it is a noble and merciless asceticism, which would root out of our hearts the last vestige of worship and adoration, lest the old gods should return and terrify us again.

For my part, I cling to this final religion, and discover in it a content and stimulus more lasting than came from the devotional ecstasies of youth. How natural it seemed to greet the great Indian poet Rabindranath Tagore by that title which so long had been given him by his countrymen, *Gurudeva* ("Revered Master")—for why should we stand reverent before waterfalls and mountaintops, or a summer moon on a quiet sea, and not before the highest miracle of all: a man who is both great and good? So many of us are mere talents, clever children in the play of life, that when genius stands in our presence we can only bow down before it as an act of God, a continuance of creation. Such men are the very life-blood of history, to which politics and industry are but frame and bones.

Part cause of the dry scholasticism from which we were suffering when James Harvey Robinson summoned us to humanize our knowledge was the conception of history as an impersonal flow of figures and "facts," in which genius played so inessential a role that histories prided themselves upon ignoring them. It was to Karl Marx above all that this theory of history was due; it was bound up with a view of life that distrusted the exceptional man, envied superior talent, and exalted the humble as the inheritors of the earth. In the end men began to write history as if it had never been lived at all, as if no drama had ever walked through it; no comedies or tragedies of struggling or frustrated men. The vivid narratives of Gibbon and Taine gave way to ash-heaps of irrelevant erudition in which every fact was correct, documented—and dead.

No, the real history of man is not in prices and wages, nor in elections and battles, nor in the even tenor of the common man; it is in the lasting contributions made by geniuses to the sum of human civilization and culture. The history of France is not, if one may say it with all courtesy, the history of the French people; the history of those nameless men and women who tilled the soil, cobbled the shoes, cut the cloth, and peddled the goods (for these things have been done everywhere and always)—the history of France is the record of her exceptional men and women, her inventors, scientists, statesmen, poets, artists, musicians, philosophers, and saints, and of the additions which they made to the technology and wisdom, the artistry and decency, of their people and mankind. And so with every country, so with the world; its history is properly the history of its great men. What are the rest of us but willing brick and mortar in their hands, that they may make a race a little finer than ourselves? Therefore I see history not as a dreary scene of politics and carnage, but as the struggle of man through genius with the obdurate inertia of matter and the baffling mystery of mind; the struggle to understand, control, and remake himself and the world.

I see men standing on the edge of knowledge, and holding the light a little farther ahead; men carving marble into forms ennobling men; men molding peoples into better instruments of greatness; men making a language of music and music out of language; men dreaming of finer lives—and living them. Here is a process of creation more vivid than in any myth; a godliness more real than in any creed.

To contemplate such men, to insinuate ourselves through study into some modest discipleship to them, to watch them at their work and warm ourselves at the fire that consumes them, this is to recapture some of the thrill that youth gave us when we thought, at the altar or in the confessional, that we were touching or hearing God. In that dreamy youth we believed that life was evil, and that only death could usher us into paradise. We were wrong; even now, while we live, we may enter it. Every great book, every work of revealing art, every record of a devoted life is a call and an open sesame to the Elysian Fields. Too soon we extinguished the flame of our hope and our reverence.

Let us change the icons, and light the candles again.

Chapter Two

The Ten "Greatest" Thinkers

WHAT IS THOUGHT? It baffles description because it includes everything through which it might be defined. It is the most immediate fact that we know, and the last mystery of our being. All other things come to us as its forms, and all human achievements find in it their source and their goal. Its appearance is the great turning point in the drama of evolution.

When did the miracle begin? Perhaps when the great surges of ice came down relentlessly from the Pole, chilling the air, destroying vegetation almost everywhere, eliminating countless species of helpless and unadaptable animals, and pushing a few survivors into a narrow tropical belt, where for generations they clung to the equator, waiting for the wrath of the North to melt. Probably it was in those critical days, when all the old and wonted ways of life were nullified by the invading ice, and inherited or traditional patterns of behavior found no success in an environment where everything was altered, that animals with comparatively complete but inflexible instinctive equipment were weeded out because they could not change within to meet the change outside; while the animal we call man, dowered with a precarious plasticity, learned and rose to an unquestioned supremacy over all the species of the forest and the field.

It was on some such life-and-death emergency as this, presumably, that human reasoning began. That same incompleteness and adaptability of native reactions which we see today in the infant, which makes it so inferior to a newborn animal but leaves it in recompense the possibility of learning—that same plasticity saved man and the higher mammals; while powerful organisms like the mammoth and the mastodon, that had prowled about hitherto supreme, succumbed to the icy change and became mere sport for paleontological curiosity. They shivered and passed away, while man, puny man, remained. Thought and invention began: the bewilderment of baffled instinct begot the first timid hypotheses, the first tentative putting together of two and two, the first generalizations, the first painful studies of similarities of quality and regularities of sequence, the first adaptation of things learned to situations so novel that reactions instinctive and immediate broke down in utter failure. It was then that certain instincts of action evolved into modes of thought and instruments of intelligence: what had been watchful waiting or stalking a prey became attention; fear and flight became caution and deliberation; pugnacity and assault became curiosity and analysis; manipulation became experiment. The animal stood up erect and became man, slave still to a thousand circumstances, timidly brave before countless perils, but in his precarious way destined henceforth to be lord of the earth.

The Adventure of Human Reason

From that obscure age to our own place and time the history of civilization has been the adventure of human reason. At every step on the stairway of progress it was thought that lifted us, slowly and tentatively, to a larger power and a higher life. If ideas do not determine history, inventions do; and inventions are determined by ideas. Certainly it is desire, the restlessness of our insatiable wants, that agitates us into thinking; but however motivated or inspired, it is thought that finds a way. We need not settle then the ancient dispute between those hero-worshipers, like Carlyle and Nietzsche, who interpret history in terms of great men, and those hero-scorners who, like Spencer and Marx, see only economic causes behind historical events; we may be sure that no pressure of economic circumstance would ever have sufficed to advance mankind if the illuminating spark of thought had not intervened.

Perhaps Tarde and James are right, and all history is a succession of inventions made by genius and turned into conventions by the people, a series of initiatives taken by adventurous leaders and spread among the masses of mankind by the waves of imitation. There is no doubt that at the beginning and summit of every age some heroic genius stands, the voice and index of his time, the inheritor and interpreter of the past, the guide and pioneer into the future. If we could find in each epoch of unfolding civilization the representative and dominating figure in its thought, we should have a living panorama of our history. But as we face the task of selecting these persons of the drama, about whom the play revolves, a dozen difficulties daunt us. What shall be our test of greatness? How, in the roster of human genius, shall we know whom to omit and whom to name?

The Criteria

Well, we shall be ruthless and dogmatic here; and though it break our hearts we shall admit no hero to our list whose thought, however subtle or profound, has not had an enduring influence upon mankind. This must be our supreme test. We shall try to take account of the originality and scope, the veracity and depth, of each thinker's thought; but what we must bear in mind above all is the extent and persistence of his influence upon the lives and minds of men. Only so can we control in some measure our personal prejudices, and arrive at some moderate impartiality in our choice.

And now how shall we define a "thinker"? Presumably the word will embrace philosophers and scientists—but only these? Shall we include men like Euripides, or Lucretius, or Dante, or Leonardo, or Shakespeare, or Goethe? No; we shall bow humbly to such great names and class them, despite the reach and fathom of their thought, as only secondarily thinkers, as artists first and above all. Shall we include such immensely influential leaders as Jesus, or Buddha, or Augustine, or Luther? No; these founders and renewers of religion would overlap our term; it was not thought or reason, but feeling and noble passion, a mystic vision and an incorrigible faith that made them, from their little foot of earth, move the world. Shall we admit into our council of ten those great men of action whose names ring down the corridor of history—men like Pericles, or Alexander, or Caesar, or Charlemagne, or Cromwell, or Napoleon, or Lincoln? No; if we spread the word "thinker" to catch such heroes in its net we shall deprive it of its distinctive meaning, and shall fail to catch the significance of thought. We must embrace within it philosophers and scientists alone. We shall seek for those men who by their thinking, rather than by their action or their passion, have most influenced mankind. We shall search for them in the quiet places of the world, far from the madding crowd; in those obscure corners where great thoughts came to them "as on dove's feet," and where for a moment they saw, as in a transfiguration, the countenance of truth. Who then shall be first?

1. CONFUCIUS At once our doubts and quarrels begin. By what canon shall we include Confucius and omit Buddha and

Christ? By this alone: that he was a moral philosopher rather than a preacher of religious faith; that his call to the noble life was based upon secular motives rather than upon supernatural considerations; that he far more resembles Socrates than Jesus.

Born (552 B.C.) in an age of confusion, in which the old power and glory of China had passed into feudal disintegration and factional strife, Kung-fu-tse undertook to restore health and order to his country. How? Let him speak:

> The illustrious ancients, when they wished to make clear and to propagate the highest virtues in the world, put their states in proper order. Before putting their states in proper order, they regulated their families. Before regulating their families, they cultivated their own selves. Before cultivating their own selves, they perfected their souls. Before perfecting their souls, they tried to be sincere in their thoughts. Before trying to be sincere in their thoughts, they extended to the utmost their knowledge. Such investigation of knowledge lay in the investigation of things, and in seeing them as they really were. When things were thus investigated, knowledge became complete. When knowledge was complete, their thoughts became sincere. When their thoughts were sincere, their souls became perfect. When their souls were perfect, their own selves became cultivated. When their selves were cultivated, their families became regulated. When their families were regulated, their states came to be put into proper order. When their states were in proper order, then the whole world became peaceful and happy.

Here is a sound moral and political philosophy within the compass of a paragraph. It was a highly conservative system; it exalted manners and etiquette, and scorned democracy; despite its clear enunciation of the Golden Rule it was nearer to Stoicism than to Christianity. A pupil having asked him should one return good for evil, Confucius replied: "With what then will you recompense kindness? Return good for good, and for evil, justice." He did not believe that all men were equal; it seemed to him that intelligence was not a universal gift. As his pupil Mencius put it: "That whereby man differs from the lower animals is little. Most people throw it away." The greatest fortune of a people would be to keep ignorant persons from public office, and secure their wisest men to rule them.

A great city, Chung-tu, took him at his word and made him magistrate. "A marvelous reformation," we are told, "ensued in the manners of the people. . . . There was an end of crime. . . . Dishonesty and dissoluteness hid their heads. Loyalty and good faith became the characteristic of the men, chastity and docility of the women." It is too good to be true, and probably it did not last very long. But even in his lifetime Confucius' followers understood his greatness and foresaw the timeless influence he was to have in molding the courtesy and poise and placid wisdom of the Chinese. "His disciples buried him with great pomp. A multitude of them built huts near his grave and remained there, mourning as for a father, for nearly three years. When all the others were gone, Tse-Kung," who had loved him beyond the rest, "continued by the grave for three years more, alone."

2 . PLATO And now we are faced with new problems. Whole civilizations confront us in which we can find no dominating name, no powerful secular personality voicing and forming his people with thought. It is so in India, and among the Jews, and among the nomad races of Asia Minor's "Fertile Crescent": we have a Buddha, an Isaiah, a Jesus, and a Mohammed, but we have no world-scientist, no world-philosopher. And in another case—perhaps the most lasting and marvelous civilization the world

has ever known—we have a hundred Pharaohs, and innumerable relics of a varied art, but no name stands out as that of one who brought the past into the perspective of wisdom and stamped his influence upon the intellectual development of his nation. We have to pass respectfully by these peoples and these centuries, and consider the glory of Periclean Greece.

Why do we love Plato? Because Plato himself was a lover: lover of comrades, lover of the intoxication of dialectical revelry, passionate seeker of the elusive reality behind thoughts and things. We love him for his unstinted energy, for the wild nomadic play of his fancy, for the joy which he found in life in all its unredeemed and adventurous complexity. We love him because he was alive every minute of his life, and never ceased to grow; such a man can be forgiven for whatever errors he has made. We love him because of his high passion for social reconstruction through intelligent control; because he retained throughout his eighty years that zeal for human improvement which is for most of us the passing luxury of youth; because he conceived philosophy as an instrument not merely for the interpretation but for the remolding of the world. We love him because he worshiped beauty as well as truth, and gave to ideas the living movement of drama, and clothed them in all the radiance of art. Here in the *Republic* and the *Dialogues* is such a riotous play of the creative imagination as might have made a Shakespeare; here is imagery squandered with lordly abandon; here is humor such as one misses in our ponderous modern philosophers; here is no system but all systems; here is one abounding fountainhead of European thought; here is prose as strong and beautiful as the great temples where Greek joy disported itself in marble; here literary prose is born, and born adult.

Plato, then, must be our second name. But we shall have to defend him against a very reasonable challenge: What of old

Socrates, almost the father, and surely the greatest martyr, of philosophy? It will seem ridiculous to omit him from a list which will include heroes not half so great as he. The reader must not be shocked to learn that Socrates is half a myth, and only half a man. A learned Frenchman, M. Dupreel (in *La Legende Socratique*), has reduced the noble gadfly to the misty historical status of Achilles, Oedipus, Romulus, and Siegfried. No doubt when we are dead some careful and conscientious scholar will prove that we never existed. But we may be certain that in good measure Socrates owes his fame as a philosopher to the creative imagination of Plato, who used the magnificent idler as the mouthpiece of his views. How much of Plato's Socrates was Socrates, and how much of it was Plato, we shall probably never know. Let us take Plato as implying both.

His *Dialogues* are among the precious possessions of mankind. Here for the first time philosophy took form, and by the very exuberance of youth achieved a perfection unrivaled in after days. Do you wish to hear noble discourse of love and friendship?—read the *Lysis,* the *Charmides,* and the *Phaedrus.* Would you know what a great and tender soul—the Platonic Socrates—thought of another life?—read the *Phaedo,* whose final pages are one of the peaks in the history of prose. Are you interested in the puzzles of the mind, in the mystery of knowledge?—read the *Parmenides* and the *Theaetetus.* Are you interested in anything?—read the *Republic:* here you shall find metaphysics, theology, ethics, psychology, theory of education, theory of statesmanship, theory of art; here you shall find feminism and birth-control, communism and socialism with all their virtues and their difficulties, eugenics and libertarian education, aristocracy and democracy, vitalism and psychoanalysis—what shall you not find here? No wonder Emerson awarded to the *Republic* the words which the occasionally pious

Omar had written of the *Koran:* "Burn the libraries, for their value is in this book."

As to Plato's influence, how can we doubt? Consider the Academy which he founded, the first and longest-lived of the universities of the world. Consider the perpetual revival of Plato's philosophy from the Neo-Platonists of Alexandria to the Cambridge Platonists of England. Consider the permeation of Christian theology with Platonic thought and symbolism, and the dominance of Plato in the culture of the earlier Middle Ages. Consider the enthusiastic Platonism of the Renaissance, when Lorenzo's table recaptured some of the glory of the *Symposium,* and Pico della Mirandola burned candles devoutly before the Master's image. Consider that at this moment, in a hundred countries and a thousand cities, a hundred thousand students, young and old, are absorbed in the *Republic* or the *Dialogues,* are being slowly and gratefully molded into a sensitive wisdom by the ardor and subtlety of Plato. Here is an immortality of the soul which makes almost insignificant the passing of the flesh.

3 . ARISTOTLE All the world would agree that Aristotle must be in our list. The Middle Ages called him *The Philosopher,* as if to say that he embodied the type at the summit of its perfection. It is not that we love him; the texts he has left behind him expound so monotonously a passionless moderation that after feeling the radiance of Plato, we freeze at the touch of the Stagyrite's tempered mind. But it is unfair to rate him by his books; we know now that they were but hasty notes made sometimes by himself, sometimes by his students, for the guidance or remembrance of his lectures; it would be absurd to judge him by comparing these technical fragments with the vivid dialogues through which Plato won for the first time a public audience for philosophy.

But let us once overcome this barrier of scholastic terminology and scornfully concentrated thought, and we shall find ourselves in the presence of an intellect of almost unbelievable depth and range. Here is a circumnavigation of the globe such as no mind has accomplished since; here every problem in science and philosophy has its consideration, its illumination, and a defensible solution; here knowledge is brought together as if through a thousand spies, and coordinated into a united vision of the world. Here the phraseology of philosophy is born, and today it is hardly possible to think without using the mintage of Aristotle's brain. Here is wisdom: calm, temperate, and well nigh complete, as of a limitless intelligence majestically overspreading life. Here are new sciences, founded with almost casual ease, as if these supreme creations of the human intellect were but the recreations of a philosopher; here it is that biology appears, and embryology, and logic. Not that no man had ever thought of these matters before, but that none had controlled his thinking with patient observation, careful experiment, and systematic formulation of results. Barring astronomy and medicine, the history of science begins with the encyclopedic labors of the tireless Stagyrite.

Confucius alone has had as great an influence. Everybody knows how, at Alexandria and in Imperial Rome, the work of Aristotle became the foundation of advancing science; how in the thirteenth century his philosophical writings, brought by the invading Moors to reawakened Europe, played a fertilizing role in the development of scholastic philosophy; how the great *Summae* of that virile age were only adaptations of the *Metaphysics* and the *Organon;* how Dante placed Aristotle first among all thinkers—"master of those who know"; how Constantinople brought the last lost treasures of his thought to the eager students of the Renaissance; and how this quiet sovereignty of one man over a millennium of intellectual history came to an end only with the audacious irreverence of Occam and Ramus, the experimental science of Roger Bacon, and the innovating philosophy of Francis Bacon. We shall not find again, in this tour of the world upon which we are engaged, another name that so long inspired and enthralled the minds of men.

4. SAINT THOMAS AQUINAS So Greece flits by, and we come to Rome. Who were the great thinkers there? Lucretius first and finest of all. Yet, because his philosophy was not his own, but with modest candor was ascribed to Epicurus, and because his influence upon his own people and upon posterity was esoteric and sporadic, touching only the topmost minds, we shall have to let him stand outside our circle, consoled with his high place in the literature of the world. And as to Seneca and Epictetus and Aurelius, they too were echoes of the Greeks, adapters of Zeno's apathy to a dying Rome. The old civilization was disappearing as they wrote; the strength had gone from the sinews of its people; freemen were everywhere replaced with slaves, and the proud free cities of the past were humbled with vassalage and tribute. The master-class divided itself into wastrel Epicureans, or Spartan Stoics too militantly stern to indulge in the delights of philosophy. Suddenly the ancient edifice collapsed, and European civilization lay in ruins.

It began again when the Church healed the strife of factions with the mystic authority of the Word, and brought men back from the battlefields to a settled life. The emperors passed, the popes remained; the legions marched no longer, but the monks and missionaries of the rising faith created quietly a new order in which thought could grow once more. How long and dreary was that second adolescence of the conscious European mind! Even today we are so precariously established in enlightenment that we can yet feel, as if in memory, the fearful groping of those many years.

And then trade grew, towns graduated into cities, schools into universities; again it was possible for some portion of mankind to be freed from toil for the leisure and luxury of thought. Abelard stirred half a continent with his eloquence. Bonaventure and Anselm laid down in majestic theology the rationale of medieval faith. When the work of preparation was complete another Aristotle came, Saint Thomas of Aquino, a man who took the universe for his specialty, and flung a frail bridge of reason across the chasms between knowledge and belief. What Dante did to the hopes and fears of the Catholic Renaissance, Aquinas did for its thought: unifying knowledge, interpreting it, and focusing it all upon the great problems of life and death. The world does not follow him now, preferring a doubting Thomas to a dogmatic one, but there was a time when every intellect honored the Angelic Doctor, and every philosophy took his gigantic *Summae* as its premises. Even today, in a hundred universities, in a thousand colleges, his thought is reverenced as still sounder than science, and his philosophy is the official system of the most powerful church in Christendom. We may not love him as we have loved the rebels and the martyrs of philosophy, but because of his modest supremacy in a great century, and his vast influence upon millions and millions of mankind, we must make a place for him in our litany of thought.

No doubt some hearts will break at this selection, including the author's own. There are so many other names that one might here invoke more lovingly than Thomas's, names far more congenial to the modern world; names like Spinoza or Nietzsche, for which one may have passionate affection rather than mere intellectual respect. But if we prove unfaithful to the standards we have ourselves laid down, we may as well abandon our quest at once; our list would then be an album of favorites rather than a gallery of great minds. . . .

5. COPERNICUS And then came a voice out of Poland, saying that this earth, footstool of God and home of his redeeming pilgrimage, was a minor satellite of a minor sun. It seemed so simple a thing to say; we cannot be moved to fear or wonder by it now; we take it for granted that this soil on which we stand is a passing thing, transiently compact of elements that will disintegrate and leave not a wrack behind. But to the medieval world, whose whole philosophy had rested on the neighborly nearness of earth and God, on the constant moral solicitude of the Deity for man, this new astronomy was an atheistic blasphemy, a ruthless blow that seemed to overthrow the Jacob's ladder which faith had built between angels and men.

Copernicus' book *On the Revolutions of the Celestial Orbs* was well named, for no book in history has created a greater revolution. That pious Polish monk, sitting patiently before the baffling stars, had meant no harm; he had no suspicion of the bearings of his thought on the future of belief; he had lost himself in the search for knowledge; he was sure that all truth must be good and beautiful, and would make men free. And so, by the magic of his mathematics, he transformed a geocentric and anthropocentric universe—a world that revolved about the earth and man—into a kaleidoscope of planets and stars in which the earth seemed but a moment's precipitation of a floating nebula. Everything was changed—distances, significances, destinies. And God, who had been closer than hands and feet, who had seemed to inhabit the friendly and flowing clouds, disappeared into the far reaches of an illimitable space. It was as if the walls of a man's house had been torn down by some blind and angry wind, leaving him unsheltered in the darkness of infinity.

We do not know how profound a thinker Copernicus was, except through this immeasurable influence of his work. With him modernity begins. With him secularism begins. With him reason makes its French Revolution against a faith immemorially enthroned, and man commences his long effort to rebuild with thought the shattered palace of his dreams. Heaven becomes mere sky and space and nothingness, or it descends upon the earth and breeds visions of Utopia in the hungry hearts of men who once had hoped for Paradise. It was as in the fable Plato told, of the gods who had cared for man till he had come of age, and then had disappeared, leaving him to the devices of his own intelligence. It was as in the ancient savage days, when the Old Man of the tribe drove the young men forth and bade them seek some other soil and raise upon it their own homes and their own happiness. With the Copernican revolution man was compelled to become of age.

6. SIR FRANCIS BACON He did not falter at this sudden maturity. On the contrary, the century that followed Copernicus was one of youthful audacity and courage in every field. Little vessels began to explore the now round and limited earth; frail minds began to explore the intellectual globe, careless of dogma, unharassed by tradition, and never dreaming that mankind would fail. Oh, the zest of those bright Renaissance days, when the poverty of a thousand years was almost forgotten, and the labor of a thousand years had made men richer and bolder, scornful of barriers and bounds! The flash of those alert eyes, the rich blood in those strong frames, the warm color of their luxurious raiment, the spontaneous poetry of that impas-

sioned speech, the creative insatiable desires, the search and sweep and fearlessness of newly liberated minds—shall we ever know such days again?

Whom can we name as voice and symbol of that fermenting age? Leonardo?—painter, musician, sculptor, etcher, architect, anatomist, physiologist, physicist, inventor, engineer, chemist, astronomer, geologist, zoologist, botanist, geographer, mathematician, and philosopher! Alas, our definitions and criteria exclude him: he was (was he not?) an artist primarily, and only secondarily a philosopher or a scientist; it is by his *Last Supper* and his *Mona Lisa* that we remember him, and not by his theory of fossils, or his anticipation of Harvey, or his majestic vision of universal and everlasting Law.—Or shall it be Giordano Bruno, that forever seeking soul, unsatisfied with the finite, hungry for an immeasurable unity, impatient of divisions, sects, dogmas, and creeds, only less controllable than the winter's winds, only less fiery than Etna, and doomed by his own turbulent spirit to a martyr's death?

No; it cannot be Bruno, for there was one greater than he: "the man who rang the bell that called the wits together"; who sent out a challenge to all the lovers and servants of truth everywhere to bind themselves together in the new order and ministry of science; who proclaimed the mission of thought as no vain scholastic dispute, no empty academic speculation, but the inductive inquiry into nature's laws, the resolute extension of the mastery of man over the conditions of his life; the man who mapped out as with royal authority the unconquered fields of research, pointed a hundred sciences to their tasks, and foretold their unbelievable victories; who inspired the Royal Society of Great Britain and the great *Encyclopedie* of France, who turned men from knowledge as meditation to knowledge as remolding power; who despised worship and longed for control; who overthrew the Aristotelian logic of unobservant reason and turned the gaze of science to the self-revealing face of nature; who carried in his brave soul, beyond any other man of that spacious age, the full spirit and purpose of the modern mind. Of course it was Francis Bacon.

7. SIR ISAAC NEWTON From that day to ours the history of the European intellect has been predominantly the progress of the Baconian as against the medieval conception of the world.

Predominantly but not continuously; there are many great figures that stood aside from this main road. In Descartes the new struggles in the arms of the old, and never quite liberates itself; in the great unifying soul of Leibnitz the medieval tradition is still powerful enough to turn a mathematician into a precarious theologian; and in Immanuel Kant the voice of ancestral faith speaks amid the skepticism of the Enlightenment. Strangely bridging these two streams of thought—the scientific and the religious—stands the figure of Spinoza: polisher of lenses and God-intoxicated man; silent devotee of lonely speculation, and formulator of the metaphysics of modern science; lover of mechanics and geometry, and martyr equally with Bruno to philosophy, dying only a slower and obscurer death. Every profound mind after him has felt his power, every historian has attested the quiet depth of his wisdom. But we have bound ourselves to judge these heroes of the mind in objective terms of influence rather than by personal estimates of wisdom, and even a lover of Spinoza must confess that the healing touch of the "gentle philosopher" has fallen upon the rarer and loftier souls rather than upon the masses or even the classes of mankind. He belongs to the islanded aristocracy of thought, and the world has not mounted to him yet.

But of Sir Isaac Newton there can be no similar dispute. "Every schoolboy knows" the story of his absent-minded genius; how the great scientist, left for a moment to his own culinary wits, and told to boil an egg three minutes for his lunch, dropped his watch into the water and watched the egg while the time-piece boiled; or how the absorbed mathematician, going up to his room to change his clothes for dinner, undressed and went contentedly to bed (it would be sad if these delightful stories were not true). Not so many schoolboys know that Newton's *Principia* marked the quiet assumption, by science, of its now unchallenged mastery over modern thought; that the laws of motion and mechanics as established by Newton became the basis of all later practical advance, of that reordered surface of the earth and that extended and intenser life which are the miracles of science in our day; the discovery of gravitation illuminated the whole world of astronomy and brought the bright confusion of the stars into an almost organic unity. "Not long ago," said Voltaire, "a distinguished company were discussing the trite and frivolous question" (alas, this is an untimely quotation!), "who was the greatest man—Caesar, Alexander, Tamerlane, or Cromwell? Someone answered that without doubt it was Isaac Newton. And rightly: for it is to him who masters our minds by the force of truth, and not to those who enslave them by violence, that we owe our reverence." Even in his lifetime the world understood that Newton belonged to its heroes.

8 . VOLTAIRE It was Voltaire who introduced to France the mechanics of Newton and the psychology of Locke, and thereby began the great age of the Enlightenment. It will shock scholastic minds to see Voltaire included among the supreme thinkers of mankind; they will protest that his thought was borrowed rather

than original, and that his influence was immoral and destructive. But which of us is original except in form? What idea can we conceive today that has not enjoyed, in one garb or another, a hoary antiquity of time? It is easier to be original in error than in truth, for every truth displaces a thousand falsehoods. An honest philosopher will admit, like Santayana, that truth, in its outlines, is as old as Aristotle, and that all we need do today is to inform and vary the design with our transient needs. Did not Spinoza, profoundest of modern thinkers, take the essentials of his thought from Bruno, Maimonides, and Descartes? Did not Ramus defend, as his thesis for the doctorate, the modest proposition that everything in Aristotle is false except that which he pilfered from Plato? And did not Plato, like Shakespeare, borrow lavishly from every store, making these stolen goods his own by transforming them with beauty? Granted that Voltaire, like Bacon, "lighted his candle at every man's torch"; it remains that he made the torch burn so brightly that it enlightened all mankind. Things came to him dull and he made them radiant; things came to him obscure, and he cleansed and scoured them with clarity; things came to him in useless scholastic dress, and he clothed them in such language that the whole world could understand and profit from them. Never did one man teach so many, or with such irresistible artistry.

Was his influence destructive? Who shall say? Shall we abandon here the objectivity of judgment we proudly assumed, and reject the laughing philosopher of Ferney because his thought was different from our own? But here we have sacrificed Spinoza, though some of us swear by his philosophy; sacrificed him because his influence has been, though deep, too narrowly confined. Evidently we must ask of Voltaire, not do we accept his conclusions, but did the world accept them, did his thinking mold the educated humanity of his age and his posterity?

It did; there can be little doubt of it. Louis XVI, seeing in his Temple prison the works of Voltaire and Rousseau, said, "Those two men have destroyed France,"—meaning despotism. Perhaps the poor king did philosophy too much honor; doubtless economic causes underlay the intellectual uprising that centered in Voltaire. But just as physiological decay leads to no action unless it sends its message of pain to consciousness, so the economic and political corruption of Bourbon France might have proceeded to utter national disintegration had not a hundred virile pens brought home the state of affairs to the conscience and consciousness of their country. And in that great task Voltaire was commander-in-chief; all the rest willingly acknowledged his lead, and did his bidding proudly. Even the mighty Frederick greeted him as "the finest genius that the ages have borne."

Beneath the recrudescence of ancient beliefs amid which we live, the influence of Voltaire quietly persists. As all Europe in his century bowed to the scepter of his pen, so the great leaders of the mind in later centuries have honored him as the fountainhead of intellectual enlightenment in our time. Nietzsche dedicated one of his books to him, and drank deeply at the Voltairian spring; Anatole France formed his thought, his wit, and his style on the ninety-nine volumes which the great sage left behind him; and Brandes, aged survivor of many a battle in the war of liberation, gives some of his dying years to a forgivably idolatrous biography of the Great Emancipator of Ferney. When we forget to honor Voltaire we shall be unworthy of freedom.

9 . IMMANUEL KANT Nevertheless, there was another side to this irrepressible conflict between simple faith and honest doubt. Something remained to be said for the creeds which the Enlightenment had apparently destroyed. Voltaire himself had

retained a sincere belief in a personal Deity, and had raised "To God" a pretty chapel at Ferney. But his followers had gone beyond him, and when he died materialism had pursued every rival philosophy from the field.

Now there are two modes of approach to an analysis of the world; we may begin with matter, and then we shall be forced to deduce from it all the mystery of mind; or we may begin with mind, and then we shall be forced to look upon matter as merely a bundle of sensations. For how can we know matter except through our senses?—and what is it then for us but our idea of it? Matter, as known to us, is but a form of mind.

When Berkeley for the first time clearly announced this novel conclusion to the world, it made a stir among the pundits, and seemed to offer a splendid exit from the infidelity of the Enlightenment. Here was a chance to reassert the primacy of mind, to reduce its threatening enemy to a mere province in its realm, and so to restore the philosophical bases of religious belief and immortal hope.

The supreme figure in this idealistic development was Immanuel Kant, perfect archetype of the abstract philosopher; Kant, who traveled much in Konigsberg, and from its promenaded streets saw the starry heavens melt into a half-unreal phenomenon, transfigured by perception into a subjective thing. It was Kant who labored best to rescue mind from matter; who argued so irrefutably (because so unintelligibly) against the uses of "pure reason"; and who, by the prestidigitation of his thought, brought back to life, magician-wise, the dear beliefs of the ancient faith.

The world heard him gladly, for it felt that it could live by faith alone, and did not love a science that merely darkened its aspirations and destroyed its hopes. Throughout the nineteenth century the influence of Kant grew; time and again, when rationalism and skepticism threatened the old citadels, men fled for strength and refuge "back to Kant." Even so matter-of-fact a man as Schopenhauer, and rabid a heretic as Nietzsche, accepted him, and looked upon his reduction of the world to mere appearance as the indispensable preliminary of every possible philosophy. So vital was Kant's work that in its outlines and its bases it remains to our own day unshaken and intact; has not science itself, through Pearson, Mach, and Poincaré, admitted that all reality, all "matter," all "nature" with its "laws," are but constructs of the mind, possibly but never certainly known in their own elusive truth? Apparently Kant had won the battle against materialism and atheism, and the world could hope again.

10. CHARLES DARWIN And then Darwin came, and the war waged anew. We cannot know now what Darwin's work may finally mean in the history of mankind. But it may well be that for posterity his name will stand as a turning point in the intellectual development of our Western civilization. If Darwin was wrong, the world may forget him as it has almost forgotten Democritus and Anaxagoras; if he was right, men will have to date from 1859 the beginning of modern thought.

For what did Darwin do but offer, quietly, and with a disarming humility, a world-picture totally different from that which had contented the mind of man before? We had supposed that it was a world of order, moving under divine guidance and omnipotent intelligence to a just and perfect fulfillment in which every virtue would find at last its fit reward. But Darwin, without attacking any creed, described what he had seen. Suddenly the world turned red, and nature, which had been so fair in the autumn's colors under the setting sun, seemed to be only a scene of slaughter and strife, in which birth was an accident, and only death a certainty. "Nature" became "natural selection," that is, a struggle for existence; and not for existence merely, but for mates and power, a ruthless elimination of the "unfit" of the tenderer flowers, the gentler animals, and the kindlier men. The surface of the earth seethed with warring species and competing individuals, every organism was the prey of some larger beast; every life was lived at the expense of some other life; great "natural" catastrophes came, ice ages, earthquakes, tornadoes, droughts, pestilences, famines, wars; millions and millions of living things were "weeded out," were quickly or slowly killed. Some species and some individuals survived for a little while— this was evolution. This was nature, this was reality.

Copernicus had reduced the earth to a speck among melting clouds; Darwin reduced man to an animal fighting for his transient mastery of the globe. Man was no longer the son of God; he was the son of strife, and his wars made the fiercest brutes ashamed of their amateur cruelty. The human race was no longer the favored creation of a benevolent deity; it was a species of ape, which the fortunes of variation and selection had raised to a precarious dignity, and which in its turn was destined to be surpassed and to disappear. Man was not immortal; he was condemned to death from the hour of his birth.

Imagine the strain upon minds brought up in the tender philosophy of our youth, and forced to adapt themselves to the harsh and bloody picture of a Darwinian world. Is it any wonder that the old faith fought fiercely for its life, that for a generation "the conflict between religion and science" was bitterer than at any time since Galileo retracted and Bruno burned at the stake? And do not the victors, exhausted by the contest, sit sadly today amid the ruins, secretly mourning their triumph, secretly yearning for the old world which their victory has destroyed?

Apologies

Well, there are our ten. Shall we see them in one glance?

1. Confucius
2. Plato
3. Aristotle
4. Saint Thomas Aquinas
5. Copernicus
6. Sir Francis Bacon
7. Sir Isaac Newton
8. Voltaire
9. Immanuel Kant
10. Charles Darwin

Those whom we have omitted would make as fair a list: Democritus, Epicurus, Marcus Aurelius, Abelard, Galileo, Spinoza, Leibnitz, Schopenhauer, Spencer, Nietzsche. And consider the vast movements of thought which we have ignored—feminism, for example, with its great leaders from Mary Wollstonecraft to Susan Anthony; and socialism, with its roster of hopeful theorists from Diogenes and Zeno to Lassalle and Marx. It must be so; no list could exhaust the treasure of man's heritage or equal its infinite variety. And it is well; let us have many lists and many heroes; we cannot honor them too much, or commemorate them excessively.

Here, perhaps, is the true litany of saints; these are the names that should adorn our calendars, with those that gave new beauty to the world, or counseled it to a gentler humanity.

CHAPTER THREE

The Ten "Greatest" Poets

I DARE NOT GO on till I face the question that every logician will have asked before our quest began: "What is your test of greatness in a poet?" It is a sorry dilemma. For if I select some objective test, proudly independent of my personal likings and tastes, we shall lose the zest of adventure and surprise that might come from a gay surrender to individual preference. And the only objective test is fame or influence, but this criterion, which seemed so plausible in choosing the greatest thinkers, breaks down in the presence of poets. Who could think of rating contemporary poets according to influence or repute? Who would name the kindly and melodious Longfellow as our greatest weaver of songs merely because greater numbers listen to him gladly than will accept the jaunty heresies and experiments of Whitman? No; let me not pretend to do more here than to reveal my prejudices, to record the men who, beyond all others, have brought me that strange mixture of music, emotion, imagery, and thought, which is poetry.

1 . HOMER Many years ago, in Russia, I saw the origin of poetry. We had resolved to study the Russians in their homes and their natural environment, and we had settled down for a week on peasant fare and peasant boards in the *isba* of our

guide's family in Chernigov. On the first night of our stay the villagers looked at us with suspicion; some timid souls announced that we had come to steal their children. But on the second night they gathered outside our hut for an open-air frolic of music and dancing, and as we sat on benches or the uncut grass an old man, bearded and blind, sitting against a wall, chanted to the accompaniment of his balalaika the ancient legends of his race. It was a plaintive narrative, always ending on a minor tone that invited the leisurely continuance of the tale, like some great revolving wheel whose impetus of motion repeatedly suffices to give it another turn. And as I listened I thought I saw Homer singing to the Greeks the Fall of Troy.

In this simple and musical way, with rhythm aiding memory, man transmitted and ornamented his history before writing came. In the days of the gods, history was sublime enough for poetry; the story of human love and war, refulgent with heavenly interest from the participation of deities, lifted the accumulated narratives of many traveling bards into the epics that we know as the *Iliad* and the *Odyssey.*

"Homer" was probably one of the singers who chanted these commemorative songs; we give his name to all the poets who composed these tales, because we are at ease with unity, and dislike the fragmentariness of truth. Every nation's literature begins with such epics, "vedas," or "sagas"—*Ramayanas, Mahabharatas, Nibelungenlieds, Beowulfs,* or *Chansons de Roland;* they are as natural to a nation's childhood as to an individual's; they take the place of those patriotic histories in which one's country is always right, wins every battle, and is especially beloved of God.

It seems unimportant and irrelevant that the tale as Homer tells it is not true, that his men and women—and even some of his deities—are apparently the creatures of his lordly imagination; it is so well invented, and so vivaciously recounted, that if the facts were different, so much the worse for the facts. Beauty has its rights as well as truth; and the *Iliad* is more important than the Trojan War. Granted that Helen was but a name or an inspiring diplomatic phrase, and that the real objective of the warring Greeks was not a lovely rake but a strategic port; nevertheless, seven Troys lie buried in the earth, while Helen is an immortal synonym of loveliness, potent still to launch a hundred thousand books upon that greatest of all oceans—ink.

Nor does it matter that these ancient epics are not complex in art or thought; they were addressed to the ear, not to the mind, and to the people, not to subtle lords; they had to be understood as soon as heard, and they had to be carried onward with vigorous action. Today we lead intricate and often introverted lives, in which action as the Greeks knew it is a rare exception, found chiefly in the press and gathered from afar; man is now an animal that stops and thinks. Therefore our literature is an analysis of motives and thought; it is in mental conflict that we find the profoundest wars and the darkest tragedies. But in Homer's day life was action, and Homer was action's prophet. His verse and style are almost dictated by action; through his turbulent hexameters the story runs like some broad and powerful stream; so that (when at last we have learned the genealogy of the heroes and the gods) we are caught and held by the poem as by some swift Niagara. And yet, in the midst of the battles, comes such quiet poetry as this, fair even in our lame rendition:

> *Thus made harangue to them Hector; and roaring*
> *the Trojans applauded;*
> *Then from the yoke loos'd their war-steeds sweat-*
> *ing, and each by his chariot*
> *Tethered his horses with thongs. And then they*
> *brought from the city,*

Hastily, oxen and goodly sheep, and wine honey-
hearted. . . .
Firewood they gathered withal; and then from the
plain to the heavens
Rose on the winds the sweet savor. And these by the
highways of battle
Hopeful sat through the night, and many their
watch-fires burning.
Even as when, in the sky, the stars shine out round
the night-orb,
Wondrous to see, and the winds are laid, and the
peaks and the headlands
Tower to the view, and the glades come out, and the
glorious heaven
Stretches itself to its widest, and sparkle the stars
multitudinous,
Gladdening the heart of the toil-wearied shep-
herd——even as countless,
'Twixt the black ships and the river of Xanthus,
glittered the watch-fires
Built by the horse-taming Trojans at Ilium. . . .
Meanwhile the war-wearied horses, champing spelt
and white barley,
Close by their chariots, waited the coming of gold-
throned dawn.

(VIII, END.)

2 . "DAVID" I name "the Psalmist" next. Who he was we do not know, except that he was not David. David was a fascinating brigand who made himself rich with robbery, usurped the throne of Saul, stole other men's wives, broke every command-

ment, and is honored by posterity as the pious author of the Psalms. But these "Songs of Praise" were composed by many hands, and any hand but David's; they were accumulated through centuries by the priests of the Temple at Jerusalem; and they were brought together only 150 years before Christ, nearly a millennium after David had ceased to be.

No matter who wrote them, or when; there they are, the profoundest lyrics in literature, so vivid with ecstasy that even those who doubt all dogmas feel in the blood a strange response to their music still. It is true that they complain too much; that they echo or anticipate Job's wonder why the just should suffer so while the ruthless prosper; that they conceive the deity in a narrow and nationalistic sense; that they beg too pugnaciously for the punishment of enemies; that they coax Jehovah with fulsome praise, reproach him for negligence (X, 1; XLIV), and in general picture the God of the Jews and the Pilgrims as a Commander-in-Chief mighty and terrible in war (XII, 3; XVIII, 8, 34, 40; LXIV, 7).

And yet, amid these songs of battle, what tender lyrics of humility and sorrow:

As for man, his days are as grass; as a flower in the field, so he flourisheth. For the wind passeth over it, and it is gone; and the place thereof shall know it no more.

Never was religious feeling so powerfully or so beautifully expressed; with language that remains, in English, a model of simplicity, clarity, and strength, and in Hebrew rings out in full organ tones of majesty; with phrases that are part of the currency of our speech ("out of the mouth of babes and sucklings," "the apple of my eye," "put not your trust in princes"); with passion and imagery as rich as even the Orient can give (the rising sun "is as a bridegroom coming out of his chamber, and rejoiceth as a strong man to run a race"). These are the finest songs ever written, and immeasurably the most influential; for two thousand years men have been moved by them as never even by songs of love; no wonder they were a solace to the Jews in suffering, and to the pioneers who made America. How like a mother's lullaby, full of assurance and repose, is the most famous psalm of all:

> *The Lord is my shepherd; I shall not want.*
> *He maketh me to lie down in green pastures: he*
> *leadeth me beside the still waters.*
> *He restoreth my soul: he leadeth me in the paths of*
> *righteousness for his name's sake.*
> *Yea, though I walk through the valley of the*
>   *shadow of death,*
> *I will fear no evil: for thou art with me; thy rod*
>   *and thy staff they shall comfort me.*
> *Thou preparest a table before me in the presence of*
>   *mine enemies;*
> *thou anointest my head with oil; my cup runneth*
>   *over.*
> *Surely goodness and mercy shall follow me all the*
>   *days of my life;*
> *and I will dwell in the house of the Lord forever.*

3 . EURIPIDES And now we are back in Greece, seated in the Theater of Dionysius, ready for Euripides. Row upon row of seats in stone semicircles, rising in widening sweep up the hill that bears on its peak the Parthenon. Restless on them sit thirty thousand Athenians; loose-togaed, passionate, talkative men, alive with feelings and ideas; the keenest audience that ever heard a poet or saw a play. Down toward the front, in chairs of

carved and ornamented marble, are the officials of the city, and the priests of the tragic god. At the foot of the great amphitheater is a small slab-paved stage; behind it the actor's booth, the *skene* or "scene." Above it all, nothing but the sky and the unfailing sun. Far down, at the base of the hill, the blue Aegean smiles.

It is the year 415 B.C. Athens is deep in the Peloponnesian War, a war of Greek with Greek, shot through with all the ferocity of relatives. The reckless dramatist has chosen for his theme another war, the siege of Troy, and his friends (among whom is Socrates, who goes only to Euripides' plays) have whispered that it will reverse Homer, and show the Trojan War from the viewpoint of the defeated and destroyed. Suddenly all is quiet: from the actor's booth a figure appears, representing the God of the Sea, Poseidon; he stands uplifted by high shoes, speaks through a resounding mask, and intones the keynote of the play:

> *How are ye blind,*
> *Ye treaders down of cities, ye that cast*
> *Temples to desolation, and lay waste*
> *Tombs, the untrodden sanctuaries where lie*
> *The ancient dead; yourselves so soon to die.*

(Was it this prologue that Socrates, as story goes, applauded so long that the actor consented to repeat it?)

The Greeks have killed Hector, and taken Troy; and Talthybius comes to take Hector's wife Andromache, his sister the proud prophetess Cassandra, and his mother Hecuba, the white-haired Queen, to serve as slaves and mistresses to the Greeks. Hecuba beats her head in grief, and mourns:

> *Beat, beat the crownless head,*
> *Rend the cheek till the tears run red!*

A lying man and a pitiless
Shall be lord of me. . . .
Oh, I will think of things gone long ago,
And weave them to a song. . . .
O thou whose wound was deepest,
Thou that my children keepest,
Priam, Priam, O age-worn king,
Gather me where thou sleepest.

(TRANSLATION OF GILBERT MURRAY.)

Andromache tries to comfort her with the thought of suicide:

O mother, having ears, hear thou this word
Fear-conquering, till thy heart as mine be stirred
Without joy. To die is only not to be. . . .
And I—long since I drew my bow
Straight at the heart of good fame; and I know
My shaft hit; and for that I am the more
Fallen from peace. All that men praise us for,
I loved for Hector's sake, and sought to win,
I knew that always, be there hurt therein
Or utter innocence, to roam abroad
Hath ill report for women; so I trod
Down the desire thereof, and walked my way
In my own garden. And light words and gay
Parley of women never passed my door.
The thoughts of mine own heart—I craved no
    more—
Spake with me, and I was happy. Constantly
I brought fair silence and a tranquil eye
For Hector's greeting, and watched well the way
Of living, where to guide and where obey. . . .

> *O my Hector, best beloved,*
> *That being mine, wast all in all to me,*
> *My prince, my wise one, O my majesty*
> *Of valiance! No man's touch had ever come*
> *Near me, when thou from out my father's home*
> *Didst lead me and make me thine. . . . And thou art*
> > *dead,*
> *And I war-flung to slavery and the bread*
> *Of shame in Hellas, over bitter seas!*

Hecuba reproves her, and suggests the hope that Hector's child, Astyanax, may some day restore his fallen city. But at that moment Talthybius returns to say that the Council of the Greeks, for the security of Hellas, has decided that Astyanax must be flung to his death from the walls of Troy. Andromache, holding the child in her arms, bids it farewell:

> *Thou little thing*
> *That curlest in my arms, what sweet scents cling*
> *Around thy neck! Beloved, can it be*
> *All nothing, that this bosom cradled thee*
> *And fostered, all the weary nights wherethrough*
> *I watched upon thy sickness, till I grew*
> *Wasted with watching? Kiss me. This one time;*
> *Not ever again. Put up thine arms, and climb*
> *About my neck; now kiss me, lips to lips . . .*
> *Oh, ye have found an anguish that outstrips*
> *All tortures of the East, ye gentle Greeks!*
> *Quick; take him, drag him, cast him from the wall*
> *If cast ye will! Tear him, ye beasts, be swift!*
> *God hath undone me, and I cannot lift*
> *One hand, one hand, to save my child from death.*

Menelaus enters, looking for Helen, and vowing to kill her on sight; but when she appears, proud and unafraid, still *dia gunaikon* (goddess among women), he is drunk at once with her beauty, forgets to murder her, and bids his slaves place her "in some chamber'd galley, where she may sail the seas." Then Talthybius returns, bearing the dead body of Hector's child. Hecuba swathes the mangled baby in burial robes, and speaks to it in lines realistic even in their sentiment:

> Ah, what a death has found thee, little one! . . .
> Ye tender arms, the same dear mould have ye
> As his. . . . And dear proud lips, so full of hope
> And closed forever! What false words ye said
> At day-break, when ye crept into my bed,
> Called me kind names, and promised,
> "Grandmother, When thou art dead, I will cut close
>   my hair
> And lead out all the captains to ride by
> Thy tomb." Why didst thou cheat me so? 'Tis I,
> Old, homeless, childless, that for thee must shed
> Cold tears, so young, so miserably dead.
> Dear God! the pattering welcomes of thy feet,
> The nursing in my lap, and oh, the sweet
> Falling asleep together! All is gone.
> How should a poet carve the funeral stone
> To tell thy story true? "There lieth here
> A babe whom the Greeks feared, and in their fear
>   Slew him." Aye, Greece will bless the tale it
>   tells! . . .
> O vain is man,
> Who glorieth in his joy and hath no fears;
> While to and fro the chances of the years
> Dance like an idiot in the wind!

(She wraps the child in the burial garments.)

> *Glory of Phrygian raiment, which my thought*
> *Kept for thy bridal day with some far-sought*
> *Queen of the East, folds thee for evermore. . . .*

And over the scene of desolation the tones of the Chorus float in melancholy song:

> *Beat, beat thine head;*
> *Beat with the wailing chime*
> *Of hands lifted in time;*
> *Beat and bleed for the dead, Woe is me for the dead!*

Here is all the power of Shakespeare, without his range and subtlety, but with a social passion that moves us as nothing in all modern drama can, except the dying Lear. This is a man strong enough to speak out, brave enough—in the very fever of war—to show its futile bestiality; brave enough to show the Greeks, to the Greeks, as barbarians in victory, and their enemies as heroes in defeat. "Euripides the human," denouncer of slavery, critic and understanding defender of women, doubter of all certainties and lover of all men: no wonder the youth of Greece declaimed his lines in the streets, and captive Athenians won their freedom by reciting his plays from memory. "If I were certain that the dead have consciousness," said the dramatist Philemon, "I would hang myself to see Euripides." He had not the classic calm and objectivity of Sophocles, nor the stern sublimity of Aeschylus; he bore the same relation to these as the emotional Dostoievski to the impeccable Turgenev and the titanic Tolstoi. But it is in Dostoievski that we find our secret hearts revealed, and our secret longing understood, and it is in Euripides that Greek drama, tired of Olympus, came down to earth and dealt revealingly with the affairs of men. "Have all the nations of the world since his time," asked Goethe, "produced one dramatist worthy to hand him his slippers?" Just one.

4. LUCRETIUS Four centuries pass. We are in an old Italian villa, built by a rich nonentity named Memmius, far from the noise of Rome. Back of the house is a quiet court, walled in from the world and shaded against the burning sun. Here is a pretty picture: two lads sitting on a marble bench beside the pool, and between them their teacher, all animation and affection, reading to them some majestic and sonorous poem. Let us recline on the lawn and listen, for this is Lucretius, the greatest poet as well as the greatest philosopher of Rome, and what he reads is (says Professor Shotwell) "the most marvelous performance in all antique literature"—the *De Rerum Natura,* a poetical essay "On the Nature of Things." He is reciting an apostrophe to Love as the source of all life and all creation:

> *Thou, O Venus, art sole mistress of the nature of things, and without thee nothing rises up into the divine realms of life, nothing grows to be lovely or glad. . . . Through all the mountains and the seas, and the rushing rivers, and the leafy nests of the birds, and the plains of the bending grass, thou strikest all breasts with fond love, and drivest each after its kind to continue its race through hot desire. . . . For so soon as the spring shines upon the day, the wild herd bound over the happy pastures, and swim the rapid streams, each imprisoned by thy charms, and following thee with desire.*
>
> (TRANSLATION BY MUNRO.)

He is a strange man, this Lucretius, obviously nervous and unstable; story has it that a love-philtre has poisoned him, and left him subject to fits of melancholy and insanity. He is all sensitivity, all pride, wounded by every prick of circumstance; a man born for peace, and forced to live in the midst of Caesar's alarms; a man with the make-up of a mystic and a saint, hardening himself into a materialist and a skeptic; a lonely soul, driven into solitude by his shyness, and yet pining for companionship and affection. He is a dark pessimist, who sees everywhere two self-canceling movements—growth and decay, reproduction and destruction, Venus and Mars, life and death. All forms begin and have their end; only atoms, space, and law remain; birth is a prelude to corruption, and even this massive universe will thaw and flow back into formlessness:

> No single thing abides, but all things flow.
> Fragment to fragment clings; the things thus grow
> Until we know and name them. By degrees
> They melt, and are no more the things we know.
> Globed from the atoms falling slow or swift
> I see the suns, I see the systems lift
> Their forms; and even the systems and their suns
> Shall go back slowly to the eternal drift.
> Thou too, O Earth—thine empires, lands and seas—
> Least, with thy stars, of all the galaxies,
> Globed from the drift like these, like these thou too
> Shalt go. Thou art going, hour by hour, like these.
> Nothing abides. Thy seas in delicate haze
> Go off; those mooned sands forsake their place;
> And where they are shall other seas in turn
> Mow with their scythes of whiteness other bays.
>
> (PARAPHRASE BY MALLOCK.)

It is a sad philosophy, hardly calculated to give men courage in the face of fate; no wonder story tells how Lucretius killed himself

(55 B.C.) at the age of forty-one. What ennobles this verse for us is the sincerity of the poet, and the rugged power of the poetry. The Latin of his lines is rude yet; a generation must pass before the language of the Romans will be polished into rhythm and refinement by Cicero's vain (and Virgil's careful) pen; but the liquid fluency of the great orator, and the feminine grace of Augustus' favorite, yield to these masculine hexameters, these picturesque unwonted adjectives, these stately verbs and resounding substantives. As we listen we are transported into the Garden of Epicurus, and hear the distant laughter of Democritus, who knew what Lucretius did not know: that gaiety is wiser than wisdom.

5. LI-PO One day, at the height of his reign, the Chinese Emperor Ming Huang received ambassadors from Korea, who brought to him important messages in a dialect which none of his ministers could understand. "What!" exclaimed the emperor, "among so many magistrates, so many scholars and warriors, cannot there be found a single one who knows enough to relieve us of vexation in this affair? If in three days no one is able to decipher this letter, every one of your appointments shall be suspended." For a day the ministers consulted and fretted, fearing for their offices and their heads, then Minister Ho Chi-chang approached the throne and said: "Your subject presumes to announce to your Majesty that there is a poet of great merit called Li at his house, who is perfectly acquainted with more than one science; command him to read this letter, for there is nothing of which he is not capable."

The emperor ordered Li to present himself at court immediately, but Li refused to come—saying that he could not possibly be worthy of the task, since his essay had been rejected by the Mandarins at the last examination. The emperor soothed him by conferring upon him the title and robes of a doctor of the first rank. Li came, found his examiners among the ministers, forced them to take off his boots, and then translated the documents, which announced that Korea proposed to make war for the recovery of its freedom. Having read the message, he dictated a learned and terrifying answer, which the emperor signed, almost believing Ho, that Li was an angel descended from heaven. The Koreans sent tribute and apologies, and the emperor gave part of the tribute to Li. Li gave it to the innkeeper, for he loved wine.

Li Tai-po, the Keats of China, had discovered the world in A.D. 701. "For twenty springs," he lived "among the clouds, loving leisure and enamored of the hills." He grew in health and strength, and became practiced in the ways of love.

> *Wine of the grapes,*
> *Goblets of gold—*
> *And a pretty maid of Wu.*
> *She comes on pony-back; she is fifteen;*
> *Blue-painted eyebrows—*
> *Shoes of pink brocade—*
> *Inarticulate speech—*
> *But she sings bewitchingly well.*
> *So, feasting at the table*
> *Inlaid with tortoise shell,*
> *She gets drunk in my lap.*
> *Ah, child, what caresses*
> *Behind lily-embroidered curtains!*

And then the aftermath:

> *Fair one, when you were here, I filled the house*
> *with flowers.*

> *Fair one, now you are gone, only an empty couch is*
>   *left.*
> *On the couch the embroidered quilt is rolled up; I*
>   *cannot sleep.*
> *It is three years since you went. The perfume you*
>   *left behind haunts me still.*
> *The perfume strays about me forever; but where are*
>   *you, Beloved?*
> *I sigh——the yellow leaves fall from the branch.*
> *I weep——the dew twinkles white on the green mosses.*

He married, but made so little gold that his wife abandoned him, taking the children with her. Li-po consoled himself with the grape and traveled from city to city, earning crumbs of bread with sheaves of song. Hearing praise of the wine of Niauching, he made at once for that city, over three hundred miles of Chinese—i.e., impassable—roads. Everybody loved him, for he spoke with the same pride and friendliness to both paupers and kings. At the capital the emperor befriended him, but could not command him. Says his fellow poet Tu Fu:

> *As for Li-po, give him a jugful,*
> *He will write one hundred poems.*
> *He dozes in a wine-shop*
> *On a city street of Chang-an;*
> *And though his Sovereign calls,*
> *He will not board the Imperial barge.*
> *"Please your Majesty," says he,*
> *"I am a god of wine."*

He accepted the philosophy of Liu Ling, who desired to be followed always by two servants, one with inexhaustible wine, the other with a spade to bury him wherever he might fall; for, said Liu, "the affairs of this world are no more than duck-weed in the river." So they soon seemed to Li, for when Ming Huang lost his throne for love the poet lost a patron, and fled from Chang-an to wander again over the countryside.

> *Why do I live among the green mountains?*
> *I laugh and answer not, my soul is serene;*
> *It dwells in another heaven and earth belonging to*
>   *no man.*
> *The peach-trees are in flower, and the water flows*
>   *on.*

His last years were bitter, for he had never stopped to make money, and in the chaos of revolution and war he found no king to keep from that starvation which is the natural reward of poetry. In the end, after imprisonment, condemnation to death, pardon, and every experiment in suffering, he found his way to his childhood home, only to die three years afterward. Legend, unsatisfied with a common end for so extraordinary a soul, told how he was drowned in a river while attempting to embrace the water's reflection of the moon.

Shall we have one more of his songs?

> *My ship is built of spice-wood and has a rudder of*
>   *mulan;*
> *Musicians sit at the two ends with jeweled bamboo*
>   *flutes and pipes of gold.*
> *What a pleasure it is, with a cask of sweet wine*
>   *and singing girls beside me,*
> *To drift on the water hither and thither with the*
>   *waves!*

I am happier than the fairy of the air, who rode on
    his yellow crane,
And free as the merman who followed the sea-gulls
    aimlessly.
Now with the strokes of my inspired pen I shake the
    Five Mountains.
My poem is done, I laugh, and my delight is vaster
    than the sea.
Oh, deathless poetry! The songs of Chu-ping are
    ever glorious as the sun and moon.
While the palaces and towers of the Chu kings
    have vanished from the hills.

6. DANTE Europe was passing through her Dark Ages when China, in the T'ang and Sung dynasties, "undoubtedly stood at the very forefront of civilization," as "the most powerful, the most enlightened, the most progressive, and the best-governed empire on the face of the globe" (Murdoch). How slowly Europe recovered from her long nightmare of Roman degeneration and barbarian invasion!

But at last new cities grew, new wealth, and new poetry; from France to Persia, and from Nijni Novgorod to Lisbon, reawakened trade brought forth the flowers of literature and art. In Naishapur Omar the Tent-maker sang his *Rubaiyat* of disillusioned joy; in Paris Villon subtracted heads from bodies and added verse to verse; and in Florence, Dante met Beatrice, and was never the same again.

See him, aged nine, at a party, trying to hide in the midst of a multitude, conscious of every limb on his body and of every eye and mind in the room, wincing at the thought that such a man is stronger, and such a girl too beautiful to notice him. Suddenly

Beatrice Portinari is before him—only a girl of eight, but at once he is in love with her, to the full depth of his adolescent soul, with a love too young to think of the flesh, and yet mature enough to be flooded with devotion. "At that instant I say truly that the spirit of life, which dwells in the most secret chamber of the heart, began to tremble with such violence that it appeared fearfully in the least pulses, and, trembling, said these words: 'Behold a God stronger than I, who, coming, shall rule over me.'" So he writes years later, in an idealized account, for nothing in memory is ever so sweet as first love. And he goes on:

> *My soul was wholly given over to the thought of this most gentle lady; whereby in brief time I fell into so frail and feeble a condition, that my appearance was grievous to many of my friends. . . . And many sought to know from me that which I wished to conceal. But I, perceiving their questioning, answered that it was Love that had brought me to this pass. I spoke of Love because I bore on my face so many signs that this could not be concealed. But when they asked me, "For whom has Love thus wasted thee?" I, smiling, looked at them and said nothing.*

But Beatrice married another, and died at twenty-four, so that it was possible for Dante to love her to the end. To make this love doubly sure he married Gemma dei Donati, and had by her four children and many quarrels. He could never quite forget the face of the girl who had died before time could efface her beauty, or realized desire could dull the edge of imagery.

He plunged into politics, was defeated and exiled, and all his goods were confiscated by the state. After fifteen years of poverty and wandering, he received intimation that he might be reinstated in all his rights of citizenship and property if he would pay a fine to Florence and undergo the humiliating ceremony of "oblation" at the altar as a released prisoner. He refused with the pride of a poet. Thereupon the gentle Florentines—being Christians to a man—decreed that wherever caught, he should be burned alive. He was not caught, but spiritually he was burned alive: he could describe hell later because he went through every realm of it on earth, and if he painted Paradise less vividly, it was for lack of personal experience. He passed from city to city, hunted and friendless, time and again near to starvation.

Perhaps the poem which he now began to write saved him from madness and suicide. Nothing so cleanses the dross out of a man as the creation of beauty or the pursuit of truth, and if the two are merged in one with him, as they were with Dante, he must be purified. This bitter world was unbearable except, as Nietzsche would phrase it, to the eye that considered it a dramatic and aesthetic spectacle; to look at it as a scene to be pictured would take some of its sting away. So Dante resolved to write: he would tell, in terrible allegory, how he had gone through hell, how he had been made clean by the purgatory of suffering, and how he had won a heaven of happiness at last, under the guidance of wisdom and love. And so, aged forty-five, he set his hand to *The Divine Comedy,* the greatest poem of modern times.

"In the midway of this our life," he tells us, he stumbled through a dark forest, and then, led by Virgil, found himself before the gates of hell, reading their dour inscription: "All hope abandon, ye who enter here!" In the Italian (*"Lasciate ogni speranza, voi ch'entrate!"*), it sounds like a racking of limbs, a tearing of flesh, and a gnashing of teeth on edge. He tells how he saw all the philosophers gathered in hell, and heard Francesca da Rimini recount her love and death with Paolo; and how from these scenes of torment he passed with Virgil to Purgatory, and then, with Beatrice to guide him, into heaven. It would not have been medieval had it not been an allegory: our human life is always a hell, says the poet, until wisdom (Virgil) purges us of evil desire, and love (Beatrice) lifts us to happiness and peace.

Dante himself never knew such peace, but remained to the end an exile, dark of countenance and soul, as Giotto painted him. People remarked that he was never known to smile, and they spoke of him, in awe, as the man who had returned from hell. Broken and worn, and prematurely old, he died at Ravenna in 1321, only fifty-six years of age. Seventy-five years later Florence begged for the ashes of him whom, alive, she would have burned at the stake, but Ravenna refused. His tomb still stands as one of the great monuments of that half-Byzantine city. There, five hundred years after Dante, another exile—Byron—knelt, and understood.

7. WILLIAM SHAKESPEARE "Dante," said Voltaire, "was a madman, and his work is a monstrosity. He has many commentators, and therefore cannot be understood. His reputation will go on increasing, for no one ever reads him." And he writes: "Shakespeare, who flourished in the time of Lope de Vega . . . is a barbarian" who composed "monstrous farces called tragedies." The English of the eighteenth century agreed with the Frenchman. "Shakespeare," said Lord Shaftesbury, "is a coarse and savage mind." In 1707 one Nahum Tate wrote a drama called *Othello,* saying that he had "borrowed the idea of the play from a nameless author." Alexander Pope, being asked why Shakespeare had written such plays, answered, "One must eat." Such is fame. A man should never read his reviewers, nor be too curious about the verdict of posterity.

All the world knows Will Shakespeare's story: how he married in haste and repented without leisure, how he fled to Lon-

don, became an actor, revamped old plays with his own light and
fire, and "did" the town with wild Kit Marlowe, believing that
"all things are with more spirit chased than enjoyed"; how he
fenced with wit against Chapman and Rare Ben Jonson at the
Mermaid Tavern; how he declared war against the rising Puri-
tans, and challenged them merrily—"Dost thou think, because
thou art virtuous, there shall be no more cakes and ale?"—how
he read Plutarch, Froissart and Holinshed and learned history,
how he read Montaigne and learned philosophy; how at last
through learning, suffering, and failure he became William the
Conqueror to all the dramatists of his time, and has ruled the
English-speaking world ever since.

His rich and riotous energy was the source of his genius and
his faults; it brought him the depth and passion of his plays, and
it brought him twins and an early death. He could not even go
home to Stratford without doing mischief on the way; for always
he stopped at Mrs. Davenant's inn at Oxford (Street-ford and
Ox-ford were fording places on the stagecoach route to Ire-
land), and finally left behind him there a young William Davenant, who became a minor poet, and never complained of his
paternity. Once the boy was running to the inn when a wit
stopped him with the query, whither he was bound? "To see my
godfather, William Shakespeare," replied the lad. "My boy," said
the wit, "do not take God's name in vain."

Invited to present plays at court, he basked for a time in the
sunshine of fair ladies and brave men, and fell madly in love with
Mary Fitton, or some other "Dark Lady" of some other name.
Dame Quickly and Doll Tearsheet disappeared from his plays,
and stately Portia entered. His soul bubbled over with romance
and comedy, and his spirit frolicked in creating Viola and Rosalind
and Ariel. But love is never quite content; in its secret heart is a
poisonous anxiety, a premonition of alienation and decay. "Love,"

says Rosalind, "is merely a madness, and, I tell you, deserves a dark-house and a whip as madmen do." "By heaven!" says Biron, "I do love, and it hath taught me melancholy."

For this was the heart of Shakespeare's tragedy, and the nadir of his life, that his dearest friend, "W. H.," to whom he had addressed sonnets of limitless love, came now and stole from him the Dark Lady of his new passion. He raged, and added to the Sonnets songs of madness and doubt; he sank into a hell of suffering, gnawed his heart out with brooding grief, and laid it bare for all to see in *Hamlet, Othello, Macbeth, Timon,* and *Lear.* But his torture deepened him; now he passed from easy comedies and simple characters to complex personalities moving through intricate tragedies to black inevitable destinies. He became through despair the greatest poet of all.

What we like in him most is the madness and richness of his speech. His style is as his life was, full of energy, riot, color, and excess; "nothing succeeds like excess." It is all hurried and breathless, this style; Shakespeare wrote in haste, and never found leisure to repent. He never erased a line or read a proof; the notion that his plays would some day be read rather than performed did not enter his head. Thoughtless of the future, he wrote with unrestrained passion. Words, images, phrases and ideas rush from him in an inexhaustible and astounding flood; one wonders from what turbulent springs they pour. He has "a mint of phrases in his brain," and his fine frenzy is of imagination all compact.

No man had ever mastered language, or used it with such lordly abandon. Anglo-Saxon words, French words, Latin words, alehouse words, medical words, legal words; tripping monosyllabic lines and sonorous sesquipedalian speech; pretty ladylike euphuisms and rough idiomatic obscenities: only an Elizabethan could have dared to write such English. We have better manners now, and less power. Yes, the plots are impossible, as Tolstoi said; the puns are puerile, the errors of scholarship are un-Baconianly legion, and the philosophy is one of surrender and despair—it does not matter. What matters is that on every page is a godlike energy of soul, and for that we will forgive a man anything. Life is beyond criticism, and Shakespeare is more alive than life.

8. JOHN KEATS Let us pause for a moment, and count the great whom we have passed by unsung. First Sappho, flinging her lyric love from a Lesbian promontory; then Aeschylus and Sophocles, winning the Dionysian prize so many times oftener than Euripides; subtle Catullus, courtly Horace, lively Ovid, and mellifluous Virgil; Petrarch and Tasso, Omar-Fitzgerald, Chaucer and Villon. But this is small offense by the side of the sins we must yet commit; even Milton and Goethe are to be called but not chosen; even Blake and Burns, Byron and Tennyson, Hugo and Verlaine, Heine and Poe. Heine the imp of verse, and Poe the better half of poetry; to leave them out seems unforgivable. Tennyson, whose every song was beautiful, and Byron, whose very life was a lyric tragedy; who are the greater ones for whom these must make way? Worse yet, not to take Milton in, who wrote like princes, potentates, and powers, and made English to thunder and blare like the Hebrew of Isaiah. Worst of all, to leave Goethe aside, the very soul of Germany, who wrote in his youth like Heine, in his maturity like Euripides, and in his old age like a Gothic cathedral—confused and endlessly surprising; what good German, or good European, will put up with this? Never mind; let us sin bravely, and name not the philosopher Goethe, but the poet, John Keats.

Stricken down with consumption in 1819, Keats, after weeks

in bed, wrote to Fanny Brawne: "Now I have had opportunities of passing nights anxious and awake, I have found thoughts obtrude upon me. 'If I should die,' said I to myself, 'I have left no immortal work behind me—nothing to make my friends proud of my memory—but I have loved the principle of beauty in all things, and if I had had time I would have made myself remembered.'" "If I had had time"—this is the tragedy of all great men. Keats never wrote anything of importance after that; nevertheless, his friends are remembered because of him, and he has left behind him poems as immortal as English, and more perfect than Shakespeare. We shall say no more about him, but refresh ourselves with himself. He sings to the nightingale:

> *Darkling I listen; and, for many a time*
> *I have been half in love with easeful Death,*
> *Called him soft names in many a mused rhyme,*
> *To take into the air my quiet breath;*
> *Now more than ever seems it rich to die,*
> *To cease upon the midnight with no pain,*
> *While thou art pouring forth thy soul abroad*
> *In such an ecstasy!*
> *Still wouldst thou sing, and I have ears in vain—*
> *To thy high requiem become a sod.*

And this to Melancholy:

> *She dwells with Beauty, Beauty that must die;*
> *And Joy, whose hand is ever at his lips*
> *Bidding adieu; and aching pleasure nigh,*
> *Turning to poison while the bee-mouth sips;*
> *Ay, in the very temple of Delight,*
> *Veil'd Melancholy was her sovran shrine;*

> *Though seen of none save him whose strenuous*
>   *tongue*
> *Can burst Joy's grape against his palate fine;*
> *His soul shall taste the sadness of her might,*
> *And be among her cloudy trophies hung.*

He went from England to Italy, seeking the sun, but the storms of the sea racked his body, and the dust of the South did him no good. Time and again he spit up cupfuls of blood. He asked that letters from Fanny Brawne be kept from him; he could not bear to read them. He ceased to write to her or his friends; he had only to die. He tried to swallow poison, but Severn took it away from him. "The idea of death," said Severn, "seems his only comfort. He talks of it with delight. The thought of recovery is beyond everything dreadful to him." In the final days "his mind grew to great quietness and peace." He dictated his epitaph: "Here lies one whose name is writ in water." Repeatedly he asked the doctor: "When will this posthumous life of mine come to an end?" As the last struggle came he said: "Severn—lift me up, for I am dying. I shall die easy. Don't be frightened. Thank God it has come." It was February 23, 1821, and he was twenty-five years old. "If I had had time"!

9. PERCY BYSSHE SHELLEY When Shelley heard that Keats had died, by tubercle bacilli and the *Quarterly Review,* he sank into a long seclusion, and poured his wrath and grief into the greatest of English elegies, *Adonais.* He must have felt, with his feminine sensitivity to every wind of fate, how closely bound was his own destiny with that of Keats—how soon he, too, would fall defeated in the eternal war of poetry and fact.

For Shelley, as Sir Henry Maine would have put it, had based his life and thought on the "State of Nature," on Rousseau's dream of a Golden Age in which all men had been, or would be, equal, and he was almost physiologically hostile to that "Historical Method" which balances ideals with realities, and aspirations with history. He could not read history; it seemed to him an abominable record of miseries and crimes; in every age that he studied he sought out not the actual conduct and vicissitudes of men, but their poetry and their religion, their ideal feelings and desires; he knew Aeschylus better than he knew Thucydides; and he forgot that in Aeschylus Prometheus was bound. What could be more certain than his suffering?

He was as sensitive as his "Sensitive Plant," subject like it to quick decay while rougher fibers flourished and survived. He described himself through Julian as "Me, who am as a nerve o'er which do creep the else unfelt oppressions of this earth." No one would have thought, seeing this delicate lad, never quite adult, that he had set all England fuming with his heresies. Trelawney, meeting him for the first time, wrote: "Was it possible this mild-looking, beardless boy could be the veritable monster at war with all the world?" McCready, the painter, said that he could not portray Shelley's face, because it was "too beautiful," and too elusively so; the man's soul was elsewhere.

No one was ever more completely or exclusively a poet. He is to poets what Spenser was before Shelley came—the very embodiment of all that poetry means. "Poetry," he wrote, in his famous "Defense,"—"poetry, and the principle of Self, of which money is the visible incarnation, are the God and the Mammon of the world. . . . But it exceeds all imagination to conceive what would have been the moral condition of the world if neither Dante, Petrarch, Boccaccio, Chaucer, Shakespeare, Calderon, Lord Bacon nor Milton had ever existed; if Raphael and Michelangelo had never been born; if the Hebrew poetry had never been translated; if a revival of the study of Greek literature had never taken place; if no monuments of ancient sculpture had been handed down to us; and if the poetry of the religion of the ancient world had been extinguished together with its beliefs."

On July 8, 1822, Shelley and his friend Williams left the Casa Magni in which they were staying on the island of Lerici, and sailed in Shelley's boat, the *Ariel,* across the Bay of Spezzia to Leghorn, to meet the impoverished Leigh Hunt and his abounding family, whom Shelley had recklessly invited to Italy as his guests. The little sailboat accomplished the trip to Leghorn safely, but as they were all about to return, the skies announced a storm. Hunt decided to remain behind with his brood, and to come the next day, but Shelley insisted on returning to Lerici; Mary Shelley and Mrs. Williams had been left there alone, and would be worried if their men did not appear. As the two youths set out from the harbor the sailors on the ships they passed warned them to come back. But they sailed on.

When they failed to reach Casa Magni that night Mary Shelley knew that fate had taken her poet from her. She broke out in wild despair, and engaged a vessel early the next morning to take her to Leghorn. There she found Hunt and Byron, but no Williams or Shelley. Byron went energetically to work and had the coast searched for mile after mile. It was not till after eight days that they found the body of Williams, lying bloated and almost unrecognizable on the sands; and not for another two days did they find Shelley—all that remained of him, the flesh torn away from his bones by vultures, the face gone beyond recognition; they knew him only from the Sophocles in one pocket and the Keats in another.

The law of Tuscany required that bodies thrown up by the sea must be burnt to avoid pestilence. So Byron and Hunt and Trelawney built a pyre, and when the body was half consumed,

Trelawney snatched the heart out of the flames. The widow had the heart buried near Keats in the Protestant Cemetery at Rome, under a slab bearing the simple words, *Cor cordium*—"heart of hearts." When she died, twenty-nine years later, it was found that her copy of *Adonais* contained (in a silken covering) the ashes of her dead lover, at that page which speaks of immortality, and the hope that springs forever in defeated men.

10. WALT WHITMAN

> *Come, Muse, migrate from Greece and Ionia;*
> *Cross out, please, those immensely overpaid*
> > *accounts,*
> *That matter of Troy, and Achilles' wrath, and*
> *Aeneas', Odysseus' wanderings;*
> *Placard "Removed" and "To let" on the rocks of your*
> > *snowy Parnassus;*
> *Repeat at Jerusalem—place the notice high on*
> > *Jaffa's gate, and on Mount Moriah;*
> *The same on the walls of your Gothic European*
> > *Cathedrals, and German, French, and Spanish*
> > *castles;*
> *For know a better, fresher, busier sphere—a wide,*
> > *untried domain awaits, demands you. . . .*
> *I heard that you asked for something to prove this*
> > *puzzle, the New World,*
> *And to define America, her athletic Democracy;*
> *Therefore I send you my poems, that you behold in*
> > *them what you wanted.*

It was a great revolution in the history of literature when a man appeared who saw the elements of poetry, the scenes of the human drama, in the very life about him; who found a way to put into song the spirit of the pioneer, and who saw that there was more poetry out under the stars than in all the salons of an unnatural life. Almost for the first time a poet was to find themes worthy of noble verse in the lives of common men; he would lift the people up into literature and be a Declaration of Independence and the Rights of Man in poetry; he would incarnate not some dead ideal of Arthur or some forgotten myth of forgotten gods, but his own rough country, his own dubious democracy, his own turbulent and growing time. What Homer had been to Greece, Virgil to Rome, Dante to Italy, Shakespeare to England, he was to be for America, because he dared to see in her, with all her faults, her material of song. He made for her new life a new form of verse, as loose and irregular, as flowing and strong as himself. And so truly did he see and sing that at last he became not only the poet of democracy and America, but, by the greatness of his soul and the universality of his vision, the poet of the modern world.

"The originality of *Leaves of Grass,*" says a French critic, "is perhaps the most absolute which has ever been manifest in literature." Originality first in words: here are no delicate nuances of language, no Shelleyan cloudiness of metaphysical speech, but masculine adjectives and nouns, plain blunt words, daringly raised from the streets and the fields to poetry. ("I had great trouble in leaving out the stock poetical touches, but succeeded at last.") And then originality of form: no rhymes, except in occasional failures like "Captain, My Captain"; and no regular meter or rhythm, but only such free and varying rhythms as breathing might show, or the wind, or the sea. Above all, originality of matter: the simple approach of an admiring child to the old and unhackneyed wonders of nature ("the noiseless splash of the sunrise," "the mad pushes of waves upon the land"); the vivid identification of himself with every soul in every experience ("My voice is the wife's voice, the screech by the rail of the stairs; they fetch my man's body up, dripping and drowned"); the brave sincerity of an open mind, rejecting and loving all creeds; the frank and lusty sense of the flesh, the tang and fragrance of the open road; the defense and understanding of woman:

> *The old face of the mother of many children!*
> *Whist! I am fully content. . . .*
> *Behold a woman!*
> *She looks out from her Quaker cap—her face is*
>   *clearer and more beautiful than the sky.*
> *She sits in an armchair, under the shaded porch of*
>   *the farmhouse,*
> *The sun just shines on her old white head.*
> *Her ample gown is of cream-hued linen;*
> *Her grandsons raised the flax, and her grand-*
>   *daughters spun it with the distaff and the*
>   *wheel.*
> *The melodious character of the earth,*
> *The finish beyond which philosophy cannot go, and*
>   *does not wish to go,*
> *The justified mother of men—*

the profound synthesis of individualism and democracy; the cosmic sweep of his imagination and his sympathy, accepting all peoples and saluting the world: these were vivifying shocks to all traditions, all prejudices, all spirits caught in ancient grooves and molds; and the very protests they aroused proved their power and their necessity. All America denounced him except one man, who redeemed them with a letter that is the seal of his nobility. On July 21, 1855, Emerson wrote to Whitman:

Dear Sir,

I am not blind to the worth of the wonderful gift of "Leaves of Grass." I find it the most extraordinary piece of wit and wisdom America has yet contributed. I am very happy in reading it, as great power makes us happy. . . . I give you joy of your free and brave thought. . . . I greet you at the beginning of a great career, which yet must have had a long foreground somewhere, for such a start. I rubbed my eyes a little to see if this sunbeam were no illusion; for the solid sense of the book is a sober certainty. . . . I wish to see my benefactor, and have felt very much like striking my tasks, and visiting New York to pay you my respects.

—R. W. Emerson

Whitman is gone—but how lately! He lived when we were children; even in our time, then, there can be giants, and even America, so crass and young, can produce a poet unique and among the best. Some months ago I stood in his Camden home, where paralysis kept him an invalid for many years; and I mourned to see about me all these reminders that genius, too, must die. But then I took up his book, and read once more the lines that have always haunted me, lines that are here left as the parting word, to haunt other memories endlessly:

> *I depart as air—I shake my white locks at the run-*
> *away sun;*
> *I effuse my flesh in eddies, and drift it in lacy jags.*
> *I bequeath myself to the dirt, to grow from the grass*
> *I love;*
> *If you want me again, look for me under your boot*
> *soles.*
> *You will hardly know who I am, or what I mean;*

But I shall be good health to you nevertheless,
And filter and fiber your blood.

Failing to fetch me at first, keep encouraged;
Missing me one place, search another;
I stop somewhere, waiting for you.

Chapter Four

The One Hundred "Best" Books for an Education

If I were rich I would have many books, and I would pamper myself with bindings bright to the eye and soft to the touch, paper generously opaque, and type such as men designed when printing was very young.

I would dress my gods in leather and gold, and burn candles of worship before them at night, and string their names like beads on a rosary. I would have my library spacious and dark and cool, safe from alien sights and sounds, with slender casements opening on quiet fields, voluptuous chairs inviting communion and reverie, shaded lamps illuminating sanctuaries here and there, and every inch of the walls concealed with the mental heritage of our race. And there at any hour my hand or spirit would welcome my friends, if their souls were hungry and their hands were clean. In the center of that temple of my books I would gather the One Hundred Best of all the educative literature in the world.

I picture to myself a massive redwood table, worked out in loving detail by the artists who carved the wood for King Henry's chapel at Westminster Abbey (I must be an old reactionary, for I abominate the hard materials that make our concrete homes and iron beds and desks today, and I find something organically responsive to my affection in everything made of wood). Along the center of the table would stand a glass case protecting and yet revealing my One Hundred Best. I picture my friends treated comfortably there, occasional hours of every week, passing from volume to volume with loving leisureliness.

Will you sit down with me? Perhaps you are a college graduate, and are ready, then, to *begin* your education. Perhaps you have never had a chance to go to college, and have never considered what else our children learn there except the latest morals. They might learn many fine things if they came to it old enough, but our youngsters take so long to grow up in these complex days that they are too immature, when they enter college, to absorb or understand the treasures offered them there so lavishly. If you have studied with life rather than with courses, it may be as well; the rough tutelage of reality has ripened you into some readiness to know great men. Here at this spacious table you will prepare yourself for membership in the International of the Mind; you will be friends with Plato and Leonardo, with Bacon and Montaigne; and when you have passed through that goodly company you will be fit for the fellowship of the finest leaders of your time and place.

Can you spare an hour a day? Or, if some days are too crowded with life and duty to give you leisure for these subtler things, can you atone for such bookless evenings by an extra hour or two on those Sunday mornings when the endless newspaper consumes you to no end? Let me have seven hours a week, and I will make a scholar and a philosopher out of you; in four years you shall be as well educated as any new-fledged Doctor of Philosophy in the land.

But let us understand each other: you must not expect any material gain from this intimacy with great men. Some lucre may flow incidentally in later years from the maturity and background that you will win, but these dividends, like those of the insurance companies, are not in any way guaranteed. Indeed, you will be "losing time" from your profession or your business; if you long for millions you had better lay aside this map of the City of God, and keep your nose to the earth. And there will be blocks along the line: occasionally you will come to an obscure or lengthy book, a bad upgrade, and all your strength will have to be subpoenaed to your task. Remember that we are not making a list of the absolutely best one hundred books, no list merely of the masterpieces of *belles lettres;* we are choosing those volumes that will do most to make a man educated.

Since we wish to have orderly minds, and to avoid the chaos of desultory reading, we shall want to begin at the beginning—even with the distant stars and the antique earth, and these beginnings will be the worst obstructions in our path. *Initium dimidium facti,* said the Romans—"the start is half the deed." Let us gird up our loins and screw our courage to the sticking point for these initial hills, and the rest will be level road, with knowledge and wisdom at every milestone, and pleasant reaches of beauty everywhere. We want here not entertainment only, but education, and we want it in such order that the knowledge we win may fall into logical sequence in our memories, and give us at last that full perspective which is the source and summit of understanding.

Therefore the first books on our list—the necessary introduction to the rest—are the most terrifying of all. A thousand barbs of wit will be invited by placing *The Outline of Science* first: alas! are we to be fed on predigested food, in the fashion of an American breakfast? Worse still, *The Outline of History,* bugbear of all proper historians, is fifth on our list—this is unforgivable. Let the critic control himself; he will soon see how far these books are used as substitutes, and how far as preparation, for the best.

At the cost of a little unpleasantness we must make ourselves acquainted with the current scientific description of the world in which man has grown: we must have a little astronomical and biological background to give some modesty to our conception of the human race; we must learn the latest gossip about electrons and chromosomes, and look on for a moment while physics and chemistry transform the world.

And then, still as introductory, we pass to ourselves. It will not do to leave for the last some knowledge of the art of health; what if, after four years, we are learned and dyspeptic, philosophers in imagination, and ruins in the flesh? Let two great physicians offer us their rival theories of how to live: Dr. Clendening will tell us, with wit scandalous in a scientist, that most of the things we eat, drink, smoke, or do are well and good, and Dr. Kellogg, with no other charm than seventy years of experience and his own ruddy health, will tell us that these ancient ways are all wrong. I believe that Dr. Kellogg is usually right; but it is conceivable that both of us are usually wrong.

We have minds as well as bodies, and perhaps we should try in some measure to understand ourselves before we ponder the history of mankind. Go, then, to William James; it is true that he wrote more than a generation ago, but his *Principles of Psychology* is still the masterpiece in its field. Avoid the abbreviated edition in one volume; the longer form is easier to read. Until you have surrounded James you need not bother with such transitory psychological fashions as psychoanalysis and behaviorism, and when you have absorbed James you will be immune to these epidemics. Read actively, not passively: consider at every step whether what you read accords with your own experience, and how far it may be applied to the guidance of your own life. But if you disagree with an author, or are shocked by his heresies, read on nevertheless; toleration of differences is one mark of a gentleman. Make notes of all passages that offer help toward the reconstruction of *your* character (not someone else's character) or the achievement of *your* aims, and classify these notes in such a way that they may at any moment, and for any purpose, be ready to your hand.

Take your time with these introductory books, for you must expect a long siege before you capture these obscure and lofty outworks of wisdom's citadel. If they burden your digestion spice them with easier morsels from the list: Plutarch, for example, or Omar, or George Moore, or Rabelais, or Poe (numbers 16, 31, 32, 45, and 91); indeed, most of the books in Groups X and XI will serve as *hors d'oeuvres* or relief when other volumes oppress you with their heaviness.

Even Wells will prove a little dull at the outset; we grow a trifle weary of his reptiles and fishes, his Cro-Magnon and Neanderthal men. But we must climb up these geological periods, and wade through these paleontological remains and anthropological origins: we sharpen our teeth on these forbidding words, we take these difficulties by the bit, and harden ourselves for anything. If we are prosperous as well as brave, we shall buy a handy dictionary, such as Webster's Collegiate (avoid vast dictionaries whose size discourage their use), and we shall adorn a wall with some spacious map of the world, so that new words and old places shall have some meaning for us. Once those Wellsian chapters are finished, Sumner's *Folkways* will be enticing dessert; no one had dreamed that a professor could make sociology so fascinating.

Do you want to know how religion began, and how it grew up from superstition to philosophy? Read Frazer's *Golden Bough;* here a great scholar has brought together in one volume the lifelong researches for which the British government, honoring itself, made him a knight of the realm. Skip if you will: learn the art of seizing out of every paragraph (usually near its beginning) the "topical sentence" in which the author lays down the proposition which his paragraph hopes to prove, and if this thesis falls outside your use or interest, leap on to the next topic, or the next, until you feel that the author is talking to you. Once that knighted volume is finished, the heaviest part of your education is over; the rest will be an adventure with gods.

Why is our list henceforth historically arranged? First, because it is well to study history as it was lived and made, taking all the activities of a civilization together—economic, social, political, scientific, philosophical, religious, literary, and artistic; in this way we shall see every work of literature, philosophy, or art in its proper place, and better understand its origin and significance—perspective is all. Second, because this arrangement will let the most delightful and entertaining masterpieces alternate with ponderous instructive tomes; it will be an aid to digestion. So, after a little more of Wells, and Breasted's perfect chapter on Egypt in that excellent history of Europe, *The Human Adventure,* we shall find welcome diversion in Brian Brown's selection of bits of wisdom from Confucius, Lao-tzu, and Mencius, and the unequaled simplicity and beauty of the Bible will atone for Faure's dithyrambs on art and Dr. Williams's meaty *History of Science* (if you cannot secure this rare and excellent work, use Dampier-Whetham's *History of Science,* or Ginzburg's *The Adventure of Science*). By these rough seas we come at last to the Isles of Greece.

Here is genius almost too abundant; how shall we crowd so many giants into our little list? Let us engage guides: Breasted and Wells will show us the larger monuments, Professor Bury will unravel for us the complexities of Greek politics, and Gilbert Murray will introduce us to the greatest literature ever written. And then the geniuses themselves: Herodotus with his delightful stories, not always true; Thucydides with his realistic thinking and his classic style (the famous "Funeral Oration" composed for Pericles by Thucydides is in book 11, chapter 6); Plutarch with biographies that will make the names in Bury live on the stage of our memories; Homer with his lilting song of gods and heroes, of Helen and Penelope; Aeschylus the mighty with his picture of Prometheus chained and unrepentant, the very symbol of genius punished for advancing the race; Sophocles with a gentle wisdom won from suffering; and "Euripides the human," mourning the misfortunes of his enemies, and at last forgiving even the gods.

Here is the first and greatest period in European philosophy: Diogenes Laertius tells the story of Socrates the martyr and Plato the reformer, of Democritus the Laughing Philosopher and Aristotle the Encyclopedia, of Zeno the Stoic and Epicurus who was not an Epicurean. Plato speaks, and paints his perfect state; the immaculately reasonable Aristotle preaches the golden mean, and marries the richest girl in Greece. Williams takes up the tale, and tells how science replaced superstition; how Hippocrates became, after many centuries of Physicians, the "Father of Medicine"; and how Archimedes solved his theorems while a soldier, symbolizing the eternal opposition of war and art, stabbed him to death. Last of all, Elie Faure lets us stand by while Pheidias, with the patience that is genius, carves figures for the Parthenon, and Praxiteles chisels Aphrodite's perfect grace. When shall we see such an age again?

To understand these Greeks would in itself be a sufficient education, and indeed, a great American educator is making the experiment of giving two years of the college course, for one hundred fortunate students, to a study of Greek civilization in all its varied wealth. The Romans do not give us so much, for though they admirably laid the foundations of social order and political continuity for the nations of modern Europe, they lost themselves too much in laws and wars, in building roads and sewers and warding off encompassing barbarians, to snatch from their hard lives the quiet thought that flowers in literature, philosophy, and art. Yet even here there are gods: the greatest statesmen that ever lived, perhaps, made companionable by Plutarch's artistry; the somber Lucretius expounding in masculine verse the inescapable Nature of Things; the delicate felicity of Virgil weaving his country's legendary past into a cloth of gold; and, last of the Romans, Marcus Aurelius, meditating on the vanity of lust and power from the vantage point of an unequaled throne.

It is a tremendous and tragic story, how this great colossus bestrode all the earth with its majesty, and then through corruption and slavery slowly rotted away, until barbarian armies from without, and Oriental cults from within, brought it down to ruin. Here it is that the greatest historian of all, Edward Gibbon, begins his stately recital of *The Decline and Fall of the Roman Empire,* and plays with his mighty organ-prose a *marche funèbre* of desolation. Let us read those purple pages leisurely; life is not so important that we may not spare for this philosopher writing history the unhurried calm that we must have in order to drink in the wisdom of his comments and the music of his periods.

Gibbon is so generous that he tells the story not of dying Rome alone, but of that infancy of northern Europe which we know as the Middle Ages. Here is the rise of the Papacy to the realization of the greatest dream of Western statesmanship—the unification of Europe; here is the conversion of Constantine and the coronation of Charlemagne; here is the bloody tale of how Mohammed and his generals, leading armies hungry for booty and infuriated with theology, swept over Africa and Spain, built the civilization of Bagdad and Cordova, and sank back into the desert when the Turks, still more barbarous than themselves, poured down through the Caucasus upon the disordered West. How the Jews and the Persians prospered under Moslem sway let Maimonides and Omar attest. We shall find in Williams the noble record of Moslem achievements in mathematics and medicine, in astronomy and philosophy, and Faure will show us their unique and delicate architecture in the Alhambra at Granada, and in India's Taj Mahal.

But there were a few Christians, too, in those days. Robinson takes up *The Human Adventure,* and describes their civilization so well that we cannot spare him from our list. Dante and Chaucer sum up the age: the Canterbury Pilgrims, though on a pious mission, frolic with stories as earthy as Rabelais's; and Dante, though at war with his Church, lifts its theology to such splendor and dignity that for a moment we forget the barbarism that created Hell. Abelard doubted that theology, but very suddenly lost the manhood to stand his ground; nothing could be more pitiful and human than his weak abandonment of Heloise and doubt. If you would know how perfect, even in our styleless days, English prose can be, read George Moore's quiet narrative of this immortal love. Henry Adams tells that story too in *Mont St. Michel and Chartres,* and expounds the encyclopedic orthodoxy of Saint Thomas Aquinas, as incidents in his personally conducted tour of the great French cathedrals; here Gothic is made to talk English, and reveal itself even to Americans. And here also we come upon that unappreciated glory, Taine's *History of English Literature:* a book as scholarly in preparation and as brilliant in exposition as can be found this side of Gibbon; it took a Frenchman to explain their literature to the English.

Finally we listen to the masculine-melancholy music of the Middle Ages, and the Gregorian chant surrounds and deepens us with its flowing majesty. Cecil Gray is no perfect guide here, he is only brief, and those who love music as the highest philosophy will deviate from our list at this point and read the fourth, fifth, and sixth volumes of the Oxford *History of Music*. Life without music, as Nietzsche said, would be a mistake.

Then the Middle Ages melt away, and suddenly we stand before that full flowering of medieval art and thought, the Italian Renaissance. Mr. Wells gives us a few inadequate pages of outline, and then we abandon ourselves, for seven spacious and astounding volumes, to the lead of John Addington Symonds, who took the very breath of his ailing life, and even the latitude of his morals, from this greatest epoch of the Christian age. (If your years are too short for so extended a tour, read Burckhardt's single volume, *The Renaissance in Italy;* if you have learned to make haste slowly, read Burckhardt and Symonds, too.) Here again is a very swarm of genius: at Florence we enter the Palace of the Medici, where Pico della Mirandola is burning candles before the bust of the rediscovered Plato, and a boy called Michelangelo is carving the figure of a toothless faun; at Rome we walk the marble floors of the Vatican with Julius II and Leo X, and watch them turning the wealth and poetry of the Church to the stimulation and nourishment of every art. Vasari opens to us the studios of Botticelli, Brunelleschi, Leonardo, Raphael, and Angelo; Faure rhapsodizes on this unprecedented efflorescence of painting, statuary, and ornament; Machiavelli makes Caesar Borgia sit for the portrait of the ideal prince; Cellini abandons murder occasionally to cast his *Perseus* or make a perfect vase; Bruno and Vanini renew man's effort to understand the world with reason; Copernicus, Vesalius, and Gilbert lay the cornerstones of modern science; and Palestrina takes us aloft on the wings of song. A supreme era unfolds itself for us in every phase of its winnowed wealth.

But Luther, coming down from the cold, stern North, does not like the licentious art of sunny Italy, and in a voice heard throughout the world he calls for the return of the Church to primitive asceticism and simplicity. The princes of Germany, using the religious revolt as an instrument of policy, separate their growing realms from the Papacy, establish a multitude of independent states, and inaugurate that dynastic nationalism which is the thread of European history from the Reformation to the Revolution. National consciousness replaces religious conscience, patriotism replaces piety, and every European people has for a century its own Renaissance. It is an age of political romance: Catherine de Medici and Henry VIII, Charles V and Philip of the Armada, Elizabeth and Essex, Mary Queen of Scots and her inextricable lovers, and the Terrible Ivan. It is an epoch of giants in literature: in France Rabelais riots with all commandments and adjectives, and Montaigne discusses affairs public and privy in the greatest essays ever written; in Spain Cervantes finds one arm sufficient for writing the most famous of all novels, and Lope de Vega composes eighteen hundred plays; in London a butcher's son produces the greatest of modern dramas, and all England, as Spengler would say, is "in form." It is the springtime of the modern soul.

Scholars are wont to say that after that brilliant coming-of-age in Spain, England, and France, Europe suffered a setback, and fell from the high level of the Renaissance. In a sense it is true: the seventeenth century is an epoch of religious conflict, the period of that Thirty Years' War which ruined Germany, and that Puritan Revolution which put an end for a century to the poetic and artistic exuberance of England. But even so consider the roster of that century. It is the time of the Three Musketeers: Richelieu and Mazarin strengthen the central government of France against the feudal barons, and bequeath a united and powerful state to Louis XIV as an organized medium of security and order for the fine flower of French culture under Voltaire. La

Rochefoucauld gives finished form to the cynicism of theaters and courts; Molière fights with ridicule the hypocrisies and conceits of his people, and Pascal mingles, in passionate rhetoric, mathematics and piety. Bacon and Milton raise English prose to its highest reach, and Milton writes, in addition, some tolerable verse. It is an era of mighty systems in philosophy: Bacon, Hobbes, and Locke in England; Descartes, Spinoza, and Leibnitz on the Continent. In science it is the age of Galileo in astronomy, of Sir William Harvey in physiology, of Robert Boyle in chemistry, of Isaac Newton in everything. In painting it is a shower of stars: in Holland, Rembrandt and Franz Hals; in Flanders, Rubens and Van Dyke; in France, Poussin and Claude Lorrain; in Spain, El Greco and Velázquez. And in music, Bach is born.

Johann Sebastian Bach is one of the Olympians nearest to Jove; and you must not rest until your body and soul have trembled with the rhythmic majesty of the Mass in B Minor, and the Passion according to St. Matthew. With the old organist of Arnstadt and everywhere, who had time between masterpieces to have twenty children, music reaches one of its twin dominating peaks; not till the mad Beethoven will it scale such a height again. The eighteenth century is full of noble melody: Handel dispenses oratorios, and Haydn develops the sonata and the symphony; Gluck makes a noble accompaniment for Iphigenia's sacrifice, and Mozart, out of his sadness and his happiness, weaves such a concourse of sweet sound as makes all later compositions seem chaotic and discordant. If you wish to know "absolute music"— music relying not on stories, or pictures, or ideas, but on its own "meaningless" beauty—turn off your radio for a moment, and play the *Andante* from Mozart's Quartet in D Major.

But here we are at the eighteenth century, which Clive Bell, in his precious volumette on Civilization, rates with the age of Pericles and the Renaissance as one of the three supreme epochs in the history of culture. An age of barbaric wars, advancing science, and liberated philosophy; of baronial exploitation, fine manners, and such handsome dress as makes our forked pantaloons and incarcerating shirts seem funereal and penal. "Those who have not lived before 1789," said that brilliant piece of "mud in a silk stocking," as Napoleon called Talleyrand, "have never known the full happiness of life." Read in Sainte-Beuve's *Portraits* the lives of these gilded men; see their pictures in Watteau and Fragonard, in Reynolds, Gainsborough, and Romney; and then take with Taine and Carlyle a front seat at the fiery drama of their fall. Think of an age that could produce such historians as Gibbon and Voltaire, such philosophers as Hume and Kant, such an undertaking as the French *Encyclopedie,* such a biographer as Boswell, such a circle as Johnson, Goldsmith, Gibbon, Burke, Garrick, and Reynolds, such novelists as Fielding and Sterne, still unsurpassed in England, such an economist as Adam Smith, such a cynic as Jonathan Swift, such a woman as Mary Wollstonecraft!

And so the Revolution comes, aristocracy is guillotined, art and manners droop, truth replaces beauty, and science remakes the world nearer to its head's desire. Let Robinson tell of that Industrial Revolution which has so quickly and profoundly transformed our lives, our governments, our morals, our religions, and our philosophies; it is one of the great pivots on which history revolves. As the eighteenth century had been the age of theoretical mechanics and physics, and the next was the era of their victory in action, so the nineteenth century was the age of theoretical biology, and the twentieth will see it in triumphant operation. New conceptions of the nature of development and man dominated the scientific scene, and precipitated a war of faiths that has unsettled and saddened the Western mind. It was a century poor in sculpture, despite the unfinished Rodin, and a century full of dubious experiments in painting, from Turner's sunsets to Whistler's rain, but in music, strange to say (for who could have expected it in an age of machines?), it outsang every other epoch in history.

Here is Beethoven, passing with the turn of the century from the Mozartian simplicity of his early works through the power of the *Eroica,* the perfection of the Fifth Symphony, and the subtle delicacy of the *Emperor* Concerto and the *Kreutzer* Sonata, to the mad exuberance of the later sonatas and the *Choral* Symphony; here is Schubert, infinite store of melody, leaving unsung masterpieces by the hundred in his attic; here is the misty-melancholy Schumann, center of one of the finest love stories in truth or fiction; here is Johannes Brahms, looking like a butcher and composing like an angel, weaving harmonies profounder than any of Schumann, and yet so loyal to his memory that, though loving with full devotion the mad musician's widow (the greatest woman pianist of her time), and protecting her for forty years, he never dared to ask her hand in marriage. What a dynasty of suffering—from the dying Beethoven shaking his fist at fate, through Schubert drunk and Schumann insane, through Chopin hunted by tubercle bacilli and deserted by George Sand, to Richard Wagner, genius and charlatan, who bore indignities for half a century, and then made German kings and princes pay the piper at Bayreuth! Happier was Mendelssohn, who was too kind and simple to suffer much; and Liszt who drank fame to the last drop, till all his life was intoxication with glory; and Rossini, who preferred cooking spaghetti to composing *The Barber of Seville;* and genial Verdi, living on his Fortunatus' purse of melody, and putting a barrel-organ into every opera house in Europe. But when we pass to Russia it is melancholy that strums the strings again: the broken Moussorgsky sings of death, and the pathetic Tschaikowsky, breaking his heart over a Venus of the opera, ends his life with a cup of poison (we may be sure of this, since all respectable historians deny it).

Apparently beauty is born in suffering, and wisdom is the child of grief. The philosophers of our parent-century were almost as unhappy as the composers: they began with Schopenhauer, who wrote an encyclopedia of misery, and ended with Nietzsche, who loved life because it was a tragedy, but went insane with the thought that he might have to live again. What a pitiful sight, once more, is the invalid Buckle, who never had a healthy moment in his life, and died at forty-one before be could complete even the Introduction to his *History of Civilization in England!* The only sound man in all the list of nineteenth-century genius was old Goethe, who differed from Shelley by growing up. Read Eckermann's *Conversations with Goethe,* and treat yourself to a week's company with a mature mind. Read Part One of *Faust,* but let no historian of literature—not even the great Brandes—lure you into Part Two: it is a senile hotch-potch of nonsense worthy of Edward Lear. The only other mind comparable to Goethe's in that age was that of Napoleon, powerful instrument of imagination, energy, and will; let Ludwig tell you his story, and then read the ninety sparkling pages with which Taine analyzes the Corsican's genius in *The Modern Regime.*

Absorb every word of Taine's chapter on Byron, and then read *Childe Harold's Pilgrimage, Cain,* and two or three cantos of *Don Juan.* Do not miss the odes of Keats: they are the finest poems in the language. Verlaine and De Musset fall out of our list, because no translation can capture their wistful melody, and Heine is included despite the failure of all who have tried to transpose from one tongue to another the wit and music of his verse. Tennyson enters with *In Memoriam* and the *Idylls of the King,* but if courage failed not, his place would be given to Sir Thomas Malory, whose *Morte d'Arthur* is a stately monument of

English prose. Of Balzac, when this century of books is done, you must read a great deal, for he is almost as illuminating as life itself. Skip through *Les Miserables,* but miss not a word of Flaubert's two masterpieces (*Mme. Bovary* and *Salambo*), which the list here dishonestly groups as one with the connivance of a publisher who issues most of Flaubert in one volume. Then you may nibble at the delicacies offered you by Anatole France, who is the distilled essence of French culture and art; only *Penguin Isle* is named, but if you are a gourmand for beauty and subtlety of speech you will read twenty volumes of Anatole. Take *Pickwick Papers* and *Vanity Fair* (or take *David Copperfield* and *Henry Esmond*) leisurely, and forget our egotistic depreciation of the Victorian Age; let our time equal that in literature and then we may throw stones.

Pass from England to Scandinavia and—ignoring Ibsen's other plays—read *Peer Gynt,* the greatest poem since *Faust.* Cross over to Russia, taste the perfection of Turgenev, wander without hurry through the mountain ranges of Tolstoi's *War and Peace* (there are only seventeen hundred pages), and at last surrender yourself to Dostoievski, the greatest novelist of all. Here again every volume is precious; if you wish to be torn up to the very roots with instruction and human revelation, you will read not only *The Brothers Karamazov,* but *Crime and Punishment, The Idiot,* and *The Possessed.* After that you may come home to America.

Does the list slight some of our native heroes? But remember our youth: we have but lately passed from pioneering to commercialism, and are just beginning to emerge from commercialism into art; Whitman is our only giant yet. Thoreau is a stage in every full life, voice of that Return-to-Nature fever which burns in the blood of every youth who protests against being too quickly civilized. Emerson is a trifle thin today, and there is almost as little meat in him as in Thoreau; but those who study style must stay with him for a week. Poe, too, is a bit overrated; a man of melodious and spookish lines, a weaver of terrible tales that appeal to our bourgeois love of mystery and our tenderfoot delight in imagined pain; we are glad to suffer by proxy. We call Poe a great artist when we only mean that his biography is interesting and his sufferings attractive to us. It is always easier to love the weak than the strong; the strong do not need our love, and instinctively we look for flaws in their irritating perfection; every statue is a provocation.

And so we come to our own century, age of electricity and *Gotterdammerung,* age of the Great Madness and the Mad Peace, age of intellectual and moral change more rapid and fundamental than any epoch in history ever knew. Let Henry Adams reveal to you the secret of our time; there is no place for it here. Possibly Bergson has the answer to Adams: the mechanistic philosophy which is the basis of our pessimism is not the necessary conclusion of biology; perhaps, after all, men are not machines. Havelock Ellis, the greatest scholar of our day, seems to us something more than a machine; and as we read *Jean Christophe,* the supreme novel of our century, we catch the feeling of the artist, as against that of the scientist—the sense not of helplessness but of creation. Spengler differs from us, and will have it that our civilization is dying; if it is so, it is only because of that passion for power, and that addiction to war, which he admires with all the envy of the intellectual who thinks that he was born for action. Let Robinson and Wells (or, if you have time, Professor Fay) bare for us the origins of the First World War, that we may see how base these envied glories are in their origin, and how filthy in their result, and let our children read them too, that they may learn how wars are made, and how men may in three years retrace nearly all the steps that mankind has slowly climbed, through three thousand years, from savagery to civilization.

These are sad books, but by the time we reach the end of our list we shall be strong enough to face truth without anesthesia. We may still believe, despite all our knowledge, that the race that made Plato and Leonardo will some day grow wisdom enough to control population, to keep the seas open to food and fuel for all peoples, and all markets open for all traders and all capital, and so by some international organization graduate humanity out of war. Stranger things than that have been accomplished in the history of mankind; forty times such a marvel could not equal the incredible development of man from slime or beast to Confucius and Christ. We have merely begun.

This, then, is our Odyssey of books. Here is another world, containing the selected excellence of a hundred generations; not quite so fair and vital as this actual world of nature and human enterprise, but abounding nevertheless in unsuspected wisdom and beauty unexplored. Life is better than literature, friendship is sweeter than philosophy, and children reach into our hearts with a profounder music than comes from any symphony, but even so these living delights offer no derogation to the modest and secondary pleasures of our books.

When life is bitter, or friendship slips away, or perhaps our children leave us for their own haunts and homes, we shall come and sit at the table with Shakespeare and Goethe, and laugh at the world with Rabelais, and see its autumn loveliness with John Keats. For these are friends who give us only their best, who never answer back, and always wait our call. When we have walked with them awhile, and listened humbly to their speech, we shall be healed of our infirmities, and know the peace that comes of understanding.

THE BOOKS

The Road To Freedom:
Being One Hundred Best Books for an Education

GROUP I. INTRODUCTORY

  1. THOMSON, J. A., *The Outline of Science.* 4v.

  2. CLENDENING, LOGAN, *The Human Body.*

 *3. KELLOGG, J. H., *The New Dietetics;* pp. 1–531, 975–1011.

  4. JAMES, Wm., *Principles of Psychology.* 2v.

 *5. WELLS, H. G., *The Outline of History;* chapters 1–14.

  6. SUMNER, W. G., *Folkways.*

  7. FRAZER, SIR JAS., *The Golden Bough.* 1-vol. ed.

GROUP II. ASIA AND AFRICA

 *8. BREASTED and ROBINSON, *The Human Adventure.* 2v. Vol. 1, chs. 2–7.

  5. WELLS, chs. 15–21, 26.

  9. BROWN, BRIAN, *The Wisdom of China.*

*10. The Bible: Genesis, Exodus, Ruth, Esther, Job, Psalms, Proverbs, Ecclesiastes, Song of Solomon, Isaiah, Amos, Micah, the Gospels, Acts of the Apostles, and Epistles of St. Paul.

*11. FAURE, ELIE, *History Of Art.* 4v. Vol. I, chs. 1–3; vol. II, chs. 1–3.

 12. WILLIAMS, H. S., *History of Science.* 5v. Bk. I, chs. 1–4.

GROUP III. GREECE

  8. BREASTED and ROBINSON, vol. I, chs. 8–19.

  5. WELLS, chs. 22–25.

 13. BURY, J. B., *History of Greece.* 2v.

 14. HERODOTUS, *Histories.* (Everyman Library.)

15. THUCYDIDES, *The Peloponnesian War.* (Everyman Library.)

*16. PLUTARCH, *Lives of Illustrious Men* (esp. Lycurgus, Solon, Themistocles, Aristides, Pericles, Alcibiades, Demosthenes, Alexander).

17. MURRAY, G., *Greek Literature.*

18. HOMER, *Iliad.* Trans. Bryant. Selections.

19. HOMER, *Odyssey.* Trans. Bryant. Selections.

20. AESCHYLUS, *Prometheus Bound.* Trans. Eliz. Browning.

21. SOPHOCLES, *Oedipus Tyrannus* and *Antigone.* Trans. Young. (Everyman Library.)

22. EURIPIDES, all plays so far translated by Gilbert Murray.

23. DIOGENES LAERTIUS, *Lives of the Philosophers.*

*24. PLATO, *Dialogues.* Trans. Jowett. Esp. *The Apology of Socrates, Phaedo,* and *The Republic* (sections 327–32, 336–77, 384–85, 392–426, 433–35, 481–83, 512–20, 572–95). 1-vol. ed. by Irwin Edman.

25. ARISTOTLE, *Nicomachean Ethics.*

26. ARISTOTLE, *Politics.*

12. WILLIAMS, *History of Science,* bk. I, chs. 5–9.

11. FAURE, *History of Art,* vol. I, chs. 4–7.

GROUP IV. ROME

8. BREASTED and ROBINSON, vol. I, chs. 20–30.

5. WELLS, chs. 27–29.

16. PLUTARCH, *Lives* (esp. Cato Censor, Tiberius and Caius Gracchus, Marius, Sylla, Pompey, Cicero, Caesar, Brutus, Antony).

27. LUCRETIUS, *On the Nature of Things.* Trans. Munro. (Certain passages are admirably paraphrased in W. H. Mallock, *Lucretius on Life and Death.*)

28. VIRGIL, *Aeneid.* Trans. Wm. Morris. Selections.

*29. MARCUS AURELIUS, *Meditations.* (Everyman Library.)

12. WILLIAMS, bk. I, chs. 10–11.

11. FAURE, vol. I, ch. 8.

*30. GIBBON, E., *Decline and Fall of the Roman Empire.* 6v. (Everyman Library.) Esp. chs. 1–4, 9–10, 14, 15–24, 26–28, 30–31, 35–36, 44, 71.

GROUP V. THE AGE OF CHRISTIANITY

8. BREASTED and ROBINSON, vol. II, chs. 1–11.

5. WELLS, chs. 30–34.

30. GIBBON, chs. 37–38, 47–53, 55–59, 64–65, 68–70.

*31. OMAR KHAYYAM, *Rubaiyat.* Fitzgerald's paraphrase.

32. MOORE, GEO., *Heloise and Abelard.* 2v.

33. DANTE, *Divine Comedy.* Trans. Longfellow, or C. E. Norton.

*34. TAINE, H., *History of English Literature,* bk. I.

35. CHAUCER, G., *Canterbury Tales.* (Everyman Library.) Selections.

36. ADAMS, H., *Mont St. Michel and Chartres.*

12. WILLIAMS, bk. II, chs. 1–3.

11. FAURE, vol. II, chs. 4–9.

37. GRAY, C., *History of Music,* chs. 1–3, 5.

GROUP VI. THE ITALIAN RENAISSANCE

5. WELLS, ch. 35.

38. SYMONDS, J. A., *The Renaissance in Italy.* 7v.

39. CELLINI, B., *Autobiography.* Trans. Symonds.

40. VASARI, G., *Lives of the Painters and Sculptors.* 4v. Esp. Giotto, Brunelleschi, Botticelli, Fra Angelico, Leonardo da Vinci, Raphael, and Michelangelo.

41. HOFFDING, H., *History of Modern Philosophy.* 2v. Sections on Bruno and Machiavelli.

42. MACHIAVELLI, N., *The Prince.*

37. GRAY, chs. 6, 8.

GROUP VII. EUROPE IN THE SIXTEENTH CENTURY

8. BREASTED and ROBINSON, vol. II, chs. 13–14.

43. SMITH, P., *The Age of the Reformation.*

44. FAGUET, E., *The Literature of France;* sections on the six-teenth century.

45. RABELAIS, *Gargantua and Pantagruel.*

*46. MONTAIGNE, *Essays.* 3v. (Everyman Library.) Esp. *Of Coaches, Of the Incommodity of Greatness, Of Vanity,* and *Of Experience.*

47. CERVANTES, *Don Quixote.*

*48. SHAKESPEARE:, *Plays.* Esp. *Hamlet, Lear, Macbeth, Othello, Romeo and Juliet, Julius Caesar, Henry IV, Merchant of Venice, As You Like It, Midsummer Night's Dream, Timon of Athens,* and *The Tempest.*

34. TAINE, bk. II, chs. 1–4.

37. GRAY, chs. 4, 7.

12. WILLIAMS, bk. II, chs.4–8.

11. FAURE, vol. III, chs. 4–6.

GROUP VIII. EUROPE IN THE SEVENTEENTH CENTURY

8. BREASTED and ROBINSON, vol. II, ch. 15.

44. FAGUET, sections on the seventeenth century.

49. LA ROCHEFOUCAULD, *Reflections.*

50. MOLIERE, *Plays.* Esp. *Tartuffe, The Miser, The Misanthrope, The Bourgeois Gentleman, The Feast of the Statue (Don Juan).*

*51. BACON, F., *Essays.* All. (Everyman Library.)

52. MILTON, J., *Lycidas, L'Allegro, Il Penseroso, Sonnets, Areopagitica,* and selections from *Paradise Lost.*

12. WILLIAMS, bk.II, chs. 9–13.

41. HOFFDING, sections on Bacon, Descartes, Hobbes, Locke, Spinoza, and Leibnitz.

53. HOBBES, *Leviathan.* (Everyman Library.)

54. SPINOZA, *Ethics* and *On the Improvement of the Understanding.* (Everyman Library.)
11. FAURE, vol. IV, chs. 1–4.
37. GRAY, chs. 9–10.

GROUP IX. EUROPE IN THE EIGHTEENTH CENTURY

8. BREASTED and ROBINSON, vol. II, chs. 16–21.
5. WELLS, chs. 26–27.
44. FAGUET, sections on the eighteenth century.
55. SAINTE-BEUVE, *Portraits of the 18th Century.*
56. VOLTAIRE, *Works.* 1-vol. ed. Esp. *Candide, Zadig,* and essays on *Toleration and History.*
57. ROUSSEAU, J. J., *Confessions.*
58. TAINE, H., *Origins of Contemporary France.* 6v. Vols. I–IV.
*59. CARLYLE, *The French Revolution.* 2v. (Everyman Library.)
34. TAINE, *History of English Literature,* bk. III, chs. 4–7.
*60. BOSWELL, *Life of Samuel Johnson.* 2v. (Everyman Library.)
61. FIELDING, H., *Tom Jones.* (Everyman Library, 2v.)
62. STERNE, L., *Tristram Shandy.* (Everyman Library.)
*63. SWIFT, J., *Gulliver's Travels.* (Everyman Library.)
64. HUME, D., *Treatise on Human Nature.* 2v. (Everyman Library.) Esp. bks. II and III.
65. WOLLSTONECRAFT, MARY, *Vindication of the Rights of Woman.*
66. SMITH, ADAM, *The Wealth of Nations.* 2v. (Everyman Library.) Selections.
12. WILLIAMS, bk. II, chs. 14–15.
41. HOFFDING, sections on the eighteenth century.
11. FAURE, vol. IV, chs. 5–6.
37. GRAY, chs. 11–12.

Group X. Europe in the Nineteenth Century

8. BREASTED and ROBINSON, vol. II, chs. 22–28.

5. WELLS, chs. 38–39.

58. TAINE, *Origins of Contemporary France*. Vol. V, *The Modern Regime,* pp. 1–90.

67. LUDWIG, E., *Napoleon.*

68. BRANDES, G., *Main Currents of 19th Century Literature.* 6v.

*69. GOETHE, *Faust.*

70. ECKERMANN, *Conversations with Goethe.*

71. HEINE, *Poems.* Trans. Louis Untermeyer.

34. TAINE, *History of English Literature,* bks. IV–V.

*72. KEATS, *Poems.*

*73. SHELLEY, *Poems.*

*74. BYRON, *Poems.*

44. FAGUET, sections on the nineteenth century.

75. BALZAC, *Père Goriot.*

*76. FLAUBERT, *Works.* I-vol. ed. Esp. *Mme. Bovary* and *Salambo.*

77. HUGO, *Les Miserables.*

78. FRANCE, ANATOLE, *Penguin Isle.*

79. TENNYSON, *Poems.*

80. DICKENS, *Pickwick Papers.*

81. THACKERAY, *Vanity Fair.*

82. TURGENEV, *Fathers and Children.*

83. DOSTOIEVSKI, *The Brothers Karamazov.*

84. TOLSTOI, *War and Peace.*

85. IBSEN, *Peer Gynt.*

12. WILLIAMS, bks. III–IV.

86. DARWIN, *Descent of Man.*

41. HOFFDING, sections on the nineteenth century.

87. BUCKLE, *Introduction to the History of Civilization in England.* Esp. part I, chs. 1–5, 15.

88. SCHOPENHAUER, *Works.* I-Vol. ed.

89. NIETZSCHE, *Thus Spake Zarathustra.*

11. FAURE, vol. IV, chs. 7–8.

37. GRAY, chs. 13–17.

GROUP XI. AMERICA

*90. BEARD, C. and M., *The Rise of American Civilization.* 2v.

91. POE, *Poems and Tales.*

92. EMERSON, *Essays.*

93. THOREAU, *Walden.*

*94. WHITMAN, *Leaves of Grass.*

95. LINCOLN, *Letters and Speeches.*

GROUP XII. THE TWENTIETH CENTURY

8. BREASTED and ROBINSON, vol. II, chs. 29–30.

5. WELLS, chs. 40–41.

96. ROLLAND, R., *Jean Christophe.* 2v.

*97. ELLIS, H., *Studies in the Psychology of Sex.* Vols. I, II, III, VI.

*98. ADAMS, H., *The Education of Henry Adams.*

99. BERGSON, *Creative Evolution.*

*100. SPENGLER, O., *Decline of the West.* 2v.

---

* Books marked with a star are recommended for purchase. Number of books starred, 27; approximate cost (based upon a survey of secondhand bookstores), $90. Number of volumes in the list: 151; approximate cost (based upon a survey of secondhand bookstores), $300. Time required for reading: 4 years at 7 hours per week, 10 hours per volume.

Chapter Five

The Ten "Peaks" of Human Progress

In the year 1794 a young French aristocrat by the magnificent name of Marquis Marie Jean de Condorcet was hiding from the guillotine in a little attic room on the outskirts of Paris. There, far from any friend, lest the coming of a friend should reveal his hiding place, he wrote the most optimistic book ever penned by the hand of man, *Esquisse d'un tableau des progrès de l'esprit humain* (*A Sketch of a Tableau of the Progress of the Human Spirit*).

Eloquently he described the recent liberation of science from the shackles of superstition and gloried in the triumphs of Newton. "Given 100 years of liberated knowledge and universal free education," he said, "and all social problems will, at the close of the next century, have been solved. . . . There is no limit to progress except the duration of the globe upon which we are placed."

Having completed his little manuscript, Condorcet handed it to his hostess. Then, in the dark of the night, he fled to a distant village inn and flung his tired body upon a bed. When he awoke, he found himself surrounded by the police. Taking from his pocket a vial of poison which he had carried for this culminating chapter of his romance, Condorcet drank it to the last drop and then fell into the arms of his captors, dead.

I have never ceased to marvel that a man so placed—driven to the very last stand of hope, with all his personal sacrifices of aristocratic privilege and fortune gone for nothing, with that great revolution upon which the youth of all Europe had pinned its hopes for a better world issuing in indiscriminate suspicion and terror—should, instead of writing an epic of despondency and gloom, have written a paean to progress.

Never before had man so believed in mankind, and perhaps never again since. Search through all ancient Greek and Latin literature, and you will find no affirmatory belief in human progress. Not until the Occident brought into the Orient the virus of—the fever of—progress can you find in any Hindu or Chinese thinker any belief in the notion that man marches forward through the years. It is a relatively new idea for men to have and to hold.

Progress—A Definition

What shall we mean by "progress"? Subjective definitions will not do; we must not conceive progress in terms of one nation, or one religion, or one code of morals; an increase of kindness, for example, would alarm our young Nietzscheans. Nor may we define progress in terms of happiness, for idiots are happier than geniuses, and those whom we most respect seek not happiness but greatness. Is it possible to find an objective definition for our term—one that will hold for any individual, any group, even for any species? Let us provisionally define progress as "increasing control of the environment by life," and let us mean by environment "all the circumstances that condition the coordination and realization of desire." Progress is the domination of chaos by mind and purpose, of matter by form and will.

It need not be continuous in order to be real. There may be "plateaus" in it, Dark Ages and disheartening retrogressions, but if the last stage is the highest of all we shall say that man makes progress. And in assessing epochs and nations we must guard against loose thinking. We must not compare nations in their youth with nations in the mellowness of their cultural maturity, and we must not compare the worst or the best of one age with the selected best or worst of all the collected past. If we find that the type of genius prevalent in young countries like America and Australia tends to the executive, explorative, and scientific kind rather than to the painter of pictures or poems, the carver of statues or words, we shall understand that each age and place calls for and needs certain brands of genius rather than others, and that the cultural sort can only come when its practical predecessors have cleared the forest and prepared the way. If we find that civilizations come and go, and mortality is upon all the works of man, we shall confess the irrefutability of death, and be consoled if, during the day of our lives and our nations, we move slowly upward, and become a little better than we were. If we find that philosophers are of slighter stature now than in the days of broad-backed Plato and the substantial Socrates, that our sculptors are lesser men than Donatello or Angelo, our painters inferior to Velázquez, our poets and composers unnameable with Shelley and Bach, we shall not despair; these stars did not all shine on the same night. Our problem is whether the total and average level of human ability has increased, and stands at its peak today.

When we take a total view, and compare our modern existence, precarious and chaotic as it is, with the ignorance, superstition, brutality, cannibalism, and diseases of primitive peoples, we are a little comforted: the lowest strata of our race may still differ only slightly from such men, but above those strata thousands and millions have reached to mental and moral heights inconceivable, presumably, to the early mind. Under the complex strain of city life we sometimes take imaginative refuge in the quiet simplicity of savage days, but in our less romantic moments we know that this is a flight-reaction from our actual tasks, that this idolatry of barbarism, like so many of our young opinions, is merely an impatient expression of adolescent mal-adaptation, part of the suffering involved in the contemporary retardation of individual maturity. A study of such savage tribes as survive shows their high rate of infantile mortality, their short tenure of life, their inferior speed, their inferior stamina, their inferior will, and their superior plagues. The friendly and flowing savage is like Nature—delightful but for the insects and the dirt.

The savage, however, might turn the argument around, and inquire how we enjoy our politics and our wars, and whether we think ourselves happier than the tribes whose weird names resound in the textbooks of anthropology. The believer in progress will have to admit that we have made too many advances in the art of war, and that our politicians, with startling exceptions, would have adorned the Roman Forum in the days of Milo and Clodius. As to happiness, no man can say; it is an elusive angel, destroyed by detection and seldom amenable to measurement. Presumably it depends first upon health, secondly upon love, and thirdly upon wealth. As to wealth, we make such progress that it lies on the conscience of our intellectuals; as to love, we try to atone for our lack of depth by unprecedented inventiveness and variety. Our thousand fads of diet and drugs predispose us to the belief that we must be ridden with disease as compared with simpler men in simpler days, but this is a delu-sion. We think that where there are so many doctors there must be more sickness than before. But in truth we have not more ail-ments than in the past, but only more money; our wealth allows us to treat and cherish and master illnesses from which primitive men died without even knowing their Greek names.

The Outline Of History

Having made these admissions and modifications, let us try to see the problem of progress in a total view. When we look at history in the large we see it as a graph of rising and falling states—nations and cultures disappearing as on some gigantic film. But in that irregular movement of countries and that chaos of men, certain great moments stand out as the peaks and essence of human history, certain advances which, once made, were never lost. Step by step man has climbed from the savage to the scientist, and these are the stages of his growth:

1 . SPEECH   Think of it not as a sudden achievement, nor as a gift from the gods, but as the slow development of articulate expression, through centuries of effort, from the mating calls of animals to the lyric flights of poetry. Without words, or common nouns, that might give to particular images the ability to represent a class, generalization would have stopped in its beginnings, and reason would have stayed where we find it in the brute. Without words, philosophy and poetry, history and prose, would have been impossible, and thought could never have reached the subtlety of Einstein or Anatole France. Without words man could not have become man—nor woman woman.

2 . FIRE   Fire made man independent of climate, gave him a greater compass on the earth, tempered his tools to hardness and durability, and offered him as food a thousand things inedible before. Not least of all it made him master of the night, and shed an animating brilliance over the hours of evening and dawn. Picture the dark before man conquered it; even now the terrors

of that primitive abyss survive in our traditions and perhaps in our blood—once every twilight was a tragedy, and man crept into his cave at sunset trembling with fear. Now we do not creep into our caves until sunrise, and though it is folly to miss the sun, how good it is to be liberated from our ancient fears! This over-spreading of the night with a billion man-made stars has bright-ened the human spirit, and made for a vivacious jollity in modern life. We shall never be grateful enough for light.

3. THE CONQUEST OF THE ANIMALS   Our memories are too forgetful, and our imagination too unimaginative, to let us realize the boon we have in our security from the larger and sub-human beasts of prey. Animals are now our playthings and our helpless food, but there was a time when man was hunted as well as hunter, when every step from cave or hut was an adven-ture, and the possession of the earth was still at stake. This war to make the planet human was surely the most vital in human history; by its side all other wars were but family quarrels, achieving nothing. That struggle between strength of body and power of mind was waged through long and unrecorded years; and when at last it was won, the fruit of man's triumph—his safety on the earth—was transmitted across a thousand genera-tions, with a hundred other gifts from the past, to be part of our heritage at birth. What are all our temporary retrogressions against the background of such a conflict and such a victory?

4. AGRICULTURE   Civilization was impossible in the hunting stage; it called for a permanent habitat, a settled way of life. It came with the home and the school, and these could not be till the products of the field replaced the animals of the forest or the

herd as the food of man. The hunter found his quarry with increasing difficulty, while the woman whom he left at home tended an ever more fruitful soil. This patient husbandry by the wife threatened to make her independent of the male, and for his own lordship's sake he forced himself at last to the prose of tillage. No doubt it took centuries to make this greatest of all transitions in human history, but when at last it was made, civilization began. Meredith said that woman will be the last creature to be civilized by man. He was as wrong as it is possible to be in the limits of one sentence. For civilization came through two things chiefly: the home, which developed those social dispositions that form the psychological cement of society, and agriculture, which took man from his wandering life as hunter, herder, and killer, and settled him long enough in one place to let him build homes, schools, churches, colleges, universities, civilization. But it was woman who gave man agriculture and the home; she domesticated man as she domesticated the sheep and the pig. Man is woman's last domestic animal, and perhaps he is the last creature that will be civilized by woman. The task is just begun: one look at our menus reveals us as still in the hunting stage.

5. SOCIAL ORGANIZATION Here are two men disputing: one knocks the other down, kills him, and then concludes that he who is alive must have been right, and that he who is dead must have been wrong—a mode of demonstration still accepted in international disputes. Here are two other men disputing: one says to the other, "Let us not fight—we may both be killed; let us take our difference to some elder of the tribe, and submit to his decision." It was a crucial moment in human history! For if the answer was "No," barbarism continued; if it was "Yes," civilization planted another root in the memory of man: the replace-

ment of chaos with order, of brutality with judgment, of violence with law. Here, too, is a gift unfelt, because we are born within the charmed circle of its protection, and never know its value till we wander into the disordered or solitary regions of the earth. God knows that our congresses and our parliaments are dubious inventions, the distilled mediocrity of the land, but despite them we manage to enjoy a security of life and property which we shall appreciate more warmly when civil war or revolution reduces us to primitive conditions. Compare the safety of travel today with the robber-infested highways of medieval Europe. Never before in history was there such order and liberty as exist in England today, and may someday exist in America, when a way is found of opening municipal office to capable and honorable men. However, we must not excite ourselves too much about political corruption or democratic mismanagement: politics is not life, but only a graft upon life; under its vulgar melodrama the traditional order of society quietly persists, in the family, in the school, in the thousand devious influences that change our native lawlessness into some measure of cooperation and goodwill. Without consciousness of it, we partake in a luxurious patrimony of social order built up for us by a hundred generations of trial and error, accumulated knowledge, and transmitted wealth.

6. MORALITY   Here we touch the very heart of our problem—are men morally better than they were? So far as intelligence is an element in morals, we have improved: the average of intelligence is higher, and there has been a great increase in the number of what we may vaguely call "developed" minds. So far as character is concerned, we have probably retrogressed: subtlety of thought has grown at the expense of stability of soul; in

the presence of our fathers we intellectuals feel uncomfortably that though we surpass them in the number of ideas that we have crowded into our heads, and though we have liberated ourselves from delightful superstitions which still bring them aid and comfort, we are inferior to them in uncomplaining courage, fidelity to our tasks and purposes, and simple strength of personality.

But if morality implies the virtues exalted in the code of Christ, we have made some halting progress despite our mines and slums, our democratic corruption, and our urban addiction to lechery. We are a slightly gentler species than we were: capable of greater kindness, and of generosity even to alien or recently hostile peoples whom we have never seen. In one year (1928) the contributions of our country to private charity and philanthropy exceeded two billion dollars—which was then one half of all the money circulating in America. We still kill murderers if, as occasionally happens, we catch them and convict them, but we are a little uneasy about this ancient retributive justice of "a life for a life," and the number of crimes for which we mete out the ultimate punishment has rapidly decreased. Two hundred years ago, in Merrie England, men might be hanged by justification of the law for stealing a shilling, and people are still severely punished if they do not steal a great deal. Not that many hundred years ago miners were hereditary serfs in Scotland, criminals were legally and publicly tortured to death in France, debtors were imprisoned for life in England, and "respectable people" raided the African coast for slaves. Less than one hundred years ago our jails were dens of filth and horror, colleges for the graduation of minor criminals into major criminals; now our prisons are vacation resorts for tired murderers. We still exploit the lower strata of our working classes, but we soothe our consciences with "welfare work." Eugenics struggles to balance with artificial selection the interference of human kindliness and benevolence with that merciless elimination of the weak and the infirm which was once the mainspring of natural selection.

We think there is more violence in the world than before, but in truth there are only more newspapers; vast and powerful organizations scour the planet for crimes and scandals that will console their readers for stenography and monogamy; and all the villainy and politics of five continents are gathered upon one page for the encouragement of our breakfasts. We conclude that half the world is killing the other half, and that a large proportion of the remainder are committing suicide. But in the streets, in our homes, in public assemblies, in a thousand vehicles of transportation, we are astonished to find no murderers and no suicides, but rather a blunt democratic courtesy, and an unpretentious chivalry a hundred times more real than when men mouthed chivalric phrases, enslaved their women, and ensured the fidelity of their wives with irons while they fought for Christ in the Holy Land.

Our prevailing mode of marriage, chaotic and deliquescent as it is, represents a pleasant refinement on marriage by capture or purchase, and *le droit de seigneur*. There is less brutality between men and women, between parents and children, between teachers and pupils, than in any recorded generation of the past. The emancipation of woman and her ascendancy over man indicate an unprecedented gentility in the once murderous male. Love, which was unknown to primitive men, or was only a hunger of the flesh, has flowered into a magnificent garden of song and sentiment, in which the passion of a man for a maid, though vigorously rooted in physical need, rises like incense into the realm of living poetry. And youth, whose sins so disturb its tired elders, atones for its little vices with such intellectual eagerness and moral courage as may be invaluable when education resolves at last to come out into the open and cleanse our public life.

7 . TOOLS   In the face of the romantics, the machine-wreckers of the intelligentsia, the pleaders for a return to the primitive (dirt, chores, snakes, cobwebs, bugs), we sing the song of the tools, the engines, the machines, that have enslaved and are liberating man. We need not be ashamed of our prosperity: it is good that comforts and opportunities once confined to barons and earls have been made by enterprise the prerogatives of all; it was necessary to spread leisure—even though at first misused—before a wide culture could come. These multiplying inventions are the new organs with which we control our environment: we do not need to grow them on our bodies, as animals must; we make them and use them, and lay them aside till we need them again. We grow gigantic arms that build in a month the pyramids that once consumed a million men; we make for ourselves great eyes that search out the invisible stars of the sky, and little eyes that peer into the invisible cells of life; we speak, if we wish, with quiet voices that reach across continents and seas; we move over the land and the air with the freedom of timeless gods. Granted that mere speed is worthless: it is as a symbol of human courage and persistent will that the airplane has its highest meaning for us: long chained, like Prometheus, to the earth, we have freed ourselves at last, and now we may look the eagle in the face.

No, these tools will not conquer us. Our present defeat by the machinery around us is a transient thing, a halt in our visible progress to a slaveless world. The menial labor that degraded both master and man is lifted from human shoulders and harnessed to the tireless muscles of iron and steel; soon every waterfall and every wind will pour its beneficent energy into factories and homes, and man will be freed for the tasks of the mind. It is not revolution but invention that will liberate the slave.

8. SCIENCE In a large degree Buckle was right: we progress only in knowledge, and these other gifts are rooted in the slow enlightenment of the mind. Here in the untitled nobility of research, and the silent battles of the laboratory, is a story fit to balance the chicanery of politics and the futile barbarism of war. Here man is at his best, and through darkness and persecution mounts steadily toward the light. Behold him standing on a little planet, measuring, weighing, analyzing constellations that he cannot see; predicting the vicissitudes of earth and sun and moon; and witnessing the birth and death of worlds. Or here is a seemingly unpractical mathematician tracking new formulas through laborious labyrinths, clearing the way for an endless chain of inventions that will multiply the power of his race. Here is a bridge: a hundred thousand tons of iron suspended from four ropes of steel flung bravely from shore to shore, and bearing the passage of countless men; this is poetry as eloquent as Shakespeare ever wrote. Or consider this citylike building that mounts boldly into the sky, guarded against every strain by the courage of our calculations, and shining like diamond-studded granite in the night. Here in physics are new dimensions, new elements, new atoms, and new powers. Here in the rocks is the autobiography of life. Here in the laboratories biology prepares to transform the organic world as physics transformed matter. Everywhere you come upon them studying, these unpretentious, unrewarded men; you hardly understand where their devotion finds its source and nourishment; they will die before the trees they plant will bear fruit for mankind. But they go on.

Yes, it is true that this victory of man over matter has not yet been matched with any kindred victory of man over himself. The argument for progress falters here again. Psychology has hardly begun to comprehend, much less to control, human conduct and desire; it is mingled with mysticism and metaphysics, with psychoanalysis, behaviorism, glandular mythology, and other diseases of adolescence (careful and modified statements are made only by psychologists of whom no one ever hears; in our country the democratic passion for extreme statements turns every science into a fad). But psychology will outlive these ills and storms; it will be matured, like older sciences, by the responsibilities which it undertakes. If another Bacon should come to map out its territory, clarify the proper methods and objectives of its attack, and point out the "fruits and powers" to be won, which of us—knowing the surprises of history and the pertinacity of men—would dare set limits to the achievements that may come from our growing knowledge of the mind? Already in our day man is turning round from his remade environment, and beginning to remake himself.

9. EDUCATION More and more completely we pass on to the next generation the gathered experience of the past. It is almost a contemporary innovation, this tremendous expenditure of wealth and labor in the equipment of schools and the provision of instruction for all; perhaps it is the most significant feature of our time. Once colleges were luxuries, designed for the male half of the leisure class; today universities are so numerous that he who runs may become a Ph.D. We have not excelled the selected geniuses of antiquity, but we have raised the level and average of human knowledge far beyond any age in history. Think now not of Plato and Aristotle, but of the stupid, bigoted,

and brutal Athenian Assembly, of the unfranchised mob and its Orphic rites, of the secluded and enslaved women who could acquire education only by becoming courtesans.

None but a child would complain that the world has not yet been totally remade by these spreading schools, these teeming bisexual universities; in the perspective of history the great experiment of education is just begun. It has not had time to prove itself; it cannot in a generation undo the ignorance and superstition of ten thousand years; indeed, there is no telling but the high birth rate of ignorance, and the determination of dogma by plebiscite, may triumph over education in the end. This step in progress is not one of which we may yet say that it is a permanent achievement of mankind. But already beneficent results appear. Why is it that tolerance and freedom of the mind flourish more easily in the northern states than in the South, if not because the South has not yet won wealth enough to build sufficient schools? Who knows how much of our preference for mediocrity in office, and narrowness in leadership, is the result of a generation recruited from regions too oppressed with economic need and political exploitation to spare time for the ploughing and sowing of the mind? What will the full fruitage of education be when every one of us is schooled till twenty, and finds equal access to the intellectual treasures of the race? Consider again the instinct of parental love, the profound impulse of every normal parent to raise his children beyond himself: here is the biological leverage of human progress, a force more to be trusted than any legislation or any moral exhortation, because it is rooted in the very nature of man. Adolescence lengthens: we begin more helplessly, and we grow more completely toward that higher man who struggles to be born out of our darkened souls. We are the raw material of civilization.

We dislike education, because it was not presented to us in

our youth for what it is. Consider it not as the painful accumulation of facts and dates, but as an ennobling intimacy with great men. Consider it not as the preparation of the individual to "make a living," but as the development of every potential capacity in him for the comprehension, control, and *appreciation* of his world. Above all, consider it, in its fullest definition, as the technique of transmitting as completely as possible, to as many as possible, that technological, intellectual, moral, and artistic heritage through which the race forms the growing individual and makes him human. Education is the reason why we behave like human beings. We are hardly born human; we are born ridiculous and malodorous animals; we *become* human, we have humanity thrust upon us through the hundred channels whereby the past pours down into the present that mental and cultural inheritance whose preservation, accumulation, and transmission place mankind today, with all its defectives and illiterates, on a higher plane than any generation has ever reached before.

10. WRITING AND PRINT Again our imagination is too weak-winged to lift us to a full perspective; we cannot vision or recall the long ages of ignorance, impotence, and fear that preceded the coming of letters. Through those unrecorded centuries men could transmit their hard-won lore only by word of mouth from parent to child; if one generation forgot or misunderstood, the weary ladder of knowledge had to be climbed anew. Writing gave a new permanence to the achievements of the mind; it preserved for thousands of years, and through a millennium of poverty and superstition, the wisdom found by philosophy and the beauty carved out in drama and poetry. It bound the generations together with a common heritage; it created that Country of the Mind in which, because of writing, genius need not die.

And now, as writing united the generations, print, despite the thousand prostitutions of it, can bind the civilizations. It is not necessary any more that civilization should disappear before our planet passes away. It will change its habitat; doubtless the land in every nation will refuse at last to yield its fruit to improvident tillage and careless tenancy; inevitably new regions will lure with virgin soil the lustier strains of every race. But a civilization is not a material thing, inseparably bound, like an ancient serf, to a given spot of the earth; it is an accumulation of technical knowledge and cultural creation; if these can be passed on to the new seat of economic power the civilization does not die, it merely makes for itself another home. Nothing but beauty and wisdom deserve immortality. To a philosopher it is not indispensable that his native city should endure forever; he will be content if its achievements are handed down, to form some part of the possessions of mankind.

We need not fret, then, about the future. We are weary with too much war, and in our lassitude of mind we listen readily to a Spengler announcing the downfall of the Western world. But this learned arrangement of the birth and death of civilizations in even cycles is a trifle too precise; we may be sure that the future will play wild pranks with this mathematical despair. There have been wars before, and Man and civilization survived them; within fifteen years after Waterloo, defeated France was producing so many geniuses that every attic in Paris was occupied. Never was our heritage of civilization and culture so secure, and never was it half so rich. We may do our little share to augment it and transmit it, confident that time will wear away chiefly the dross of it, and that what is finally fair and worthy in it will be preserved, to illuminate many generations.

Chapter Six

Twelve Vital Dates in World History

THE IDEA OF CREATING a list of twelve vital dates in history came to me at Manila as I was preparing to set sail across the Pacific to America. It came at an appropriate moment, for it found me struggling with the problem of dates in working on the first volume of *The Story of Civilization*.

It was already quite clear to me that the inclusion of dates in the text would make the story as accurate and dull as a good encyclopedia; that the transformation of dead data into living narrative would require some other disposition of dates than one that would infest with them every page of the tale. The arrangement arrived at, after much pseudopodial trial and error, was to confine all dates to the margin and the notes. Perhaps some such plan would alleviate the pain inflicted by some of the textbooks of history used in our colleges and schools.

I had occasion, some years back, to examine the texts employed in certain institutions of lower learning in my neighborhood. The geography, which might have been made one of the most fascinating studies of all, was especially abominable; a mere massing of dead information, much of it made false or worthless by the war, much of it restricted to the superficial features of a nation's life, much of it made ridiculous by provincial prejudice against the Orient. But the textbook of history—Bear and Bagley's *History of the American People*—was intelligently and intelligibly written, recording the progress of civilization, as well as the logic-chopping vicissitudes of politics, and presenting its sound scholarship with pleasing artistry. It is a splendid volume.

In many high schools I have found, as the standard historical text of world history, Breasted's *Ancient Times,* which I regard as the finest schoolbook in America, and along with it, only slightly inferior to it, the books of Robinson and Beard on modern European history. In these volumes there is no excessive use of dates, and if we are to agree that dates have been overdone, we shall have to acknowledge, also, that some of our texts have avoided this fault, and many of them represent a great improvement on the class books of our younger days.

I should hardly be content to have my pupils know only twelve dates, and I presume that the choice of this baker's number would not suggest an optimum, but rather a minimum—dates, let us say, that every baker should know. How many dates a man should carry with him will depend, of course, on his functions and purposes. A farmer might do his job very well, and bring up a fine family, with no other date in his head than that of the next state fair, but a man condemned to the intellectual life, precluded from the deepening contacts of experiment and action, ought to have sufficient knowledge of man's chronology to give him, as some poor substitute for wide personal experience, that historical perspective which is one road to philosophy and understanding.

Such a man should be able to name the century (though not necessarily the precise dates) of world-transforming inventions and discoveries like gunpowder, printing, the steam engine, electricity, and the discovery of America. He should know the centuries of the world's greatest statesmen—say Hammurabi, Moses, Darius I, Solon, Pericles, Alexander, Caesar, Charles V, Louis XIV, Peter the Great, Frederick the Great, Henry VIII, Elizabeth, Disraeli, Gladstone, Bismarck, Cavour, Washington, Hamilton, Jefferson, and Lincoln; of the world's greatest scientists and philosophers—say Confucius, Socrates, Plato, Aristotle, Copernicus, Francis Bacon, Isaac Newton, Spinoza, Voltaire, Kant, Schopenhauer, and Darwin; of the world's greatest saints— say lknaton, Lao-tzu, Isaiah, Buddha, Christ, Marcus Aurelius, Augustine, Francis of Assisi, Loyola, Luther, and Gandhi.

This man of intellectual interests should also know the centuries of the world's greatest poets—say Homer, the Psalmist, Euripides, Virgil, Horace, Li-po, Dante, Shakespeare, Milton, Goethe, Pushkin, Keats, Byron, Shelley, Hugo, Poe, Whitman, and Tagore; of the world's greatest makers of music—say Palestrina, Bach, Handel, Mozart, Beethoven, Chopin, Liszt, Paganini, Brahms, Tschaikowsky, Verdi, Wagner, Paderewski, and Stravinsky; and of the world's greatest artists or works of art—say Karnak and Luxor and the Pyramids, Pheidias and Praxiteles, Wu Tao-tzu and Sesshiu and Hiroshige, Chartres and the Taj Mahal, Giotto and Dürer, Leonardo, Raphael, and Michelangelo, Titian and Correggio, El Greco and Velázquez, Rubens, Rembrandt, and Van Dyck, Reynolds and Gainsborough, Turner and Whistler, Millet and Cezanne.

I have left out the great prose writers, lest this chapter should read like a telephone directory, or a list of radical exportees, or a register of "dirty foreigners." The reader can help me by making here his own pantheon. Let him then examine his friends and himself on the centuries and work of these men (perhaps we should also add a list of great women, from Queen Hatshepsut to Madame Curie), and so rate them and himself with a new Binet-Simon test.

If, however, one is condemned to live on a mental desert island, and can take only twelve dates with him, these dates should presumably be such as to carry in their implications the essential history of mankind. About them should cluster such associations that on their docket the greater achievements of the human mind would string themselves in a concatenation of development, in an order and perspective that would clarify old knowledge and facilitate the new. Since history is varied, and all aspects of human activity in any age are bound up with the rest, many such chains of pivotal events might be composed. What follows, then, are not *the* twelve world dates; they are merely twelve.

1 . 4241 B.C.—THE INTRODUCTION OF THE EGYPTIAN CALENDAR This date alone, the earliest definite date in history, is sufficient to cause some disturbance to fiercely orthodox souls who believe, as did Bishop Ussher, that the world was created in 4004 B.C. To accept the testimony of Egyptologists that a calendar existed on the Lower Nile 237 years before the creation of the world might serve as a fertilizing shock to any virgin mind.

The implications of that calendar are endless. Consider the development of astronomy and mathematics that must have preceded its formulation. Consider how long even then a civilization must have endured to set aside from the economic life men with leisure enough to chart the stars and capture the course of the sun. It was a very sensible calendar compared with ours: it divided the year into twelve months of thirty days each, with five intercalary days at the end for roistering. And it stands in the memory for all Egypt, for three thousand years of recorded civilization, with orderly government, security of life and property, comforts for the body, delights for the senses, and instruction for the mind. It stands for Cheops, who built the greatest of the pyramids; and Thutmose III, who built Karnak; and Iknaton, who literally sold his kingdom for a song (arousing revolution by writing a monotheistic hymn); and Cleopatra, who led Antony to ruin by the nose—if one may speak so metonymically.

2. 543 B.C.—THE DEATH OF BUDDHA No other soul, I suppose, has ever been so influential. It is not so much that several hundred million men and women profess the Buddhist religion today; in truth, Buddhism does not follow Buddha, but is a mass of legends and superstitions that have no more right to use his name than the ferocious Christianity of Calvin or Torquemada or Tennessee has to use the name of Christ. But Buddha means India, for the spirit of India lies in religion rather than in science, in contemplation rather than in action, in a fraternal gentleness rather than in the application of mathematics to artillery, or of chemistry to bombs.

Life, said Buddha, is full of suffering; it can be made bearable only by doing no injury to any living thing, and speaking no evil of any man—or woman either. Let us hope that that simple religion is what lies behind the infinite superstitions of the Hindu mind today, and let us take the date of Buddha as the beginning of a civilization that has known every vicissitude, every injustice, every slavery, and yet in the midst of it has produced geniuses and saints from Buddha and Asoka to Gandhi and Tagore.

3. 478 B.C.—THE DEATH OF CONFUCIUS We must have some symbol to represent China for us—China, so gigantic in size that it calls itself "All Under Heaven," and so old that it records the doings of its kings for the last four thousand years.

I envy those Chinese schoolboys who were made to memorize every word of Confucius. I have found every line profound and applicable, and sometimes I think that if these maxims had sunk into my memory for twenty years, I might have in me a little of the poise of soul, the simple dignity, the quiet understanding, the depth of character, the infinite courtesy that I have found in the educated Chinese everywhere. Never has one man so written his name upon the face and spirit of a people as Confucius has done in China. Let us take him again as a symbol and a suggestion: behind him are the delicate lyrics of the T'ang Dynasty's poets, the mystic landscapes of the Chinese painters, the perfect vases of the Chinese potters, the secular and terrestrial wisdom of the Chinese philosophers; perhaps the greatest of all historic civilizations is summed up in his name.

4. 399 B.C.—THE DEATH OF SOCRATES When this man passed, drunk with hemlock, also passed the most astonishing picture in ancient history—the Age of Pericles. But this time I am not thinking of philosophy. Behind Socrates I see his friend and lover, Alcibiades, and the destructive tragedy of the Peloponnesian War. I see Aspasia, the learned courtesan, at whose feet the old Gadfly sat with Pericles. I see Pericles gathering rich men around him and persuading them to finance the Athenian drama. I see Euripides contending with Sophocles for the dramatic prize in the Theater of Dionysius. I see Ictinus in slow thought molding the columns of the Parthenon, and Pheidias carving the gods and heroes of its frieze. I see young Plato winning the prize at the Panathenaean games. I want some stopping-point in history that shall bring to my memory a few of the thousand facets of this brave and varied age, when for the first time a whole civilization liberated itself from superstition, and created science, drama, democracy, and liberty, and passed on to Rome and Europe half of our intellectual and aesthetic heritage.

5. 44 B.C.—THE DEATH OF CAESAR A few years before the death of Georg Brandes, the Danish critic who helped the French Taine to make the British understand English literature, an American student visited him and found him in a very somber mood. "Why are you sad?" the visitor asked. "Don't you know," answered Brandes, "that this is the anniversary of the greatest blunder in history—the assassination of Caesar?"

The old critic might have found blunders nearer home, like the defeat of Napoleon at Waterloo, and perhaps he exaggerated a little the importance of Brutus' *sottise*. For in a sense it is not Caesar whom we wish to remember; it is the succession of developments that followed upon his death: the reconstruction of Roman law and order by the statesmanlike Augustus on the basis and lines of Caesar's preliminary work, the flourishing of arts and letters under the extension of the *Pax Romana* to Rome, the poetry of Virgil and Horace, the prose of Pliny and Tacitus, the philosophy of Epictetus and Aurelius, the beneficent rule of Hadrian and Antoninus, the beautification of the Forum and the capital with architecture and statuary, the building of those roads, and the revision and codification of those laws, which were to be Rome's essential legacy to the modern world. As the death of Socrates may be used to sum up the Periclean Age of Athens, so the death of Caesar stands as the door to the Golden Age of Rome.

6. ? B.C.—THE BIRTH OF CHRIST This date the reader may place *ad lib.,* since no man knows it. For us it is the most important date of all, because it divides all history in the West, gives us our greatest hero and model, provides us with that body of myth and legend which is now passing from the theological to the literary stage, and marks the beginning of that Christian age

which seems today to be approaching its close. After us the deluge; God knows what a mess of occult faiths will in the present century replace the tender and cruel theologies that praised and dishonored Christ.

7. A.D. 632—THE DEATH OF MOHAMMED It was in this year, so designated by us infidels but known to the Mohammedans as A.H. 10 (the tenth year after the Hegira), that Mohammed left this earth, after founding the faith that was to overrun and dominate for centuries all northern Africa from Cairo to Morocco, southern Europe in Turkey and Spain, and half of Asia from Jerusalem and Bagdad to Teheran and Delhi. Even Christianity cannot boast of so many wars waged in its name, or so many heathen killed.

With this trifling exception, it was a noble religion, sternly monotheistic, rejecting images and priests and the polytheism of saints, building strong characters with the doctrine of fatalism and the discipline of war, raising great universities and cultures at Cordova, Granada, Cairo, Bagdad, and Delhi, giving the world one of its greatest rulers—Akbar of India—and ennobling Spain, Egypt, Constantinople, Palestine, and India with gracious architecture from the Alhambra to the Taj Mahal. Today, despite their political dismemberment, they are still growing in numbers and strength; in India and China they are making converts every hour of every day. There is no surety that the future is not theirs.

8. 1294—THE DEATH OF ROGER BACON This date is almost as good as any other to mark the first use of gunpowder, for the rebellious English monk who died in this year may be held partly responsible for its invention. It was Roger Bacon

who first definitely described the explosive that would revolutionize the world and offer to all pious statesmen a substitute for birth control. "One may cause to burst forth from bronze," he wrote, "thunderbolts more formidable than those produced by nature. A small quantity of prepared matter occasions a terrible explosion accompanied by brilliant light. One may multiply the phenomena so far as to destroy an army or a city."

Very likely. It was gunpowder that gave to the rising bourgeoisie of late medieval Europe the means of overthrowing the feudal baron by bombarding from a distance his once impregnable castle. It was gunpowder that made the infantry as important as the cavalry, and gave the common man a new prestige in war and a new power in revolutions. It was gunpowder that turned war from a gentleman's game, occasionally fatal, to a form of standardized mass destruction, a mode of removing from the earth, with a few minutes' bombardment, the work of a hundred thousand artists' hands laboring for three centuries. Perhaps this is the most important date in the story of the fall of man; though some cynic might argue that a still more tragic event was the invention of thinking, the liberation of intellect from instinct, the consequent separation of sex from reproduction, and the abandonment of the perpetuation of the race to the selected morons of every land.

9. 1454—THE PRESS OF JOHANNES GUTENBERG (AT MAINZ ON THE RHINE) ISSUES THE FIRST PRINTED DOCUMENTS BEARING A PRINTED DATE The Germans had used printing from movable types for some fourteen years before; the Chinese had done such printing as far back as A.D. 1041; and in 1900 a block-printed book was discovered in China which had been published in 868. Nothing is new in China,

democracy least of all. They invented gunpowder and used it chiefly for fireworks. They invented printing and never used it for tabloid newspapers, crime club fiction, or Freudian biographies.

In Western civilization, printing helped money and muskets to liberate the middle class and put an end to the rule of the knights and the priests. It enabled the people to read the Bible, and so engendered the Reformation. It immensely widened the circle to which a writer might address his ideas. And by transferring the making of books from monks to printers' devils, and the patronage of books from the aristocracy and the church to the commonalty and the laity, it made possible the propaganda and development of democracy and free thought.

Napoleon remarked that the Bourbons might have preserved themselves, and prevented the French Revolution, by maintaining a governmental monopoly of ink. Our empowered middle class has profited by the example and has made literacy an impediment to the acquisition of truth. One hardly knows, today, whether printing does more harm than good, or whether the growth of knowledge and learning has not weakened character as much as it has stocked the mind—but let us try it a little further!

10. 1492—COLUMBUS DISCOVERS AMERICA When Columbus discovered us, he put an end to the Italian Renaissance by changing trade routes from the Mediterranean to the Atlantic, and bringing wealth and power first to Spain, making possible Velázquez and Cervantes, Murillo and Calderon; then to England, financing Shakespeare, Milton, Bacon, and Hobbes; then to the Netherlands, producing Rembrandt and Spinoza, Rubens and Van Dyck, Hobbema and Vermeer; and then to France, generating Rabelais and Montaigne, Poussin and Claude

Lorraine. When, in 1564, Michelangelo died and Shakespeare was born, it was a sign that the Renaissance had died in Italy and been reborn in England. The discovery of America cooperated with the Reformation, and the diminution of Peter's Pence, in ending for a time the role of Italy in history.

Later the development of the New World opened up a vast market for European goods and a vast area for Europe's surplus population. This is the secret of Europe's rapid growth in wealth and power, and its conquest of Africa and Asia and Australia. And all the history of America, with its experiments in popular sovereignty and popular education (would that the order had been reversed), lay potential in that magnificent adventure of 1492.

11. 1769—JAMES WATT BRINGS THE STEAM ENGINE TO PRACTICAL UTILITY This event inaugurated the Industrial Revolution. Hero of Alexandria made a steam engine in 130 B.C.; Della Porta, Savery, and Newcomen had made better ones in 1601, 1698, and 1705; but it was Watt's stone that capped the arch and changed the world.

Essentially there are only two fundamental and pivotal events in human history: the Agricultural Revolution, in which men passed from hunting to tillage and settled down to build homes, schools, and civilization; and the Industrial Revolution, which threw millions and millions of men, first in England, then in America and Germany, then in Italy and France, then in far away Japan, now in China, the Soviet Union, and India, out of their homes and their farms into cities and factories. It transformed society and government by empowering the owners of machinery and the controllers of commerce beyond the owners of titles and land. It transformed religion by generating science and its persuasive miracles and inducing many men to think in terms of cause and effect and machines. It transformed the mind by substituting novel and varied stimuli, necessitating thought, for the old ancestral and domestic situations to which instinct had been adapted and sufficient. It transformed woman by taking her work from the home and forcing her into the factories to recapture it. It transformed morals by complicating economic life, postponing marriage, multiplying contacts and opportunities, liberating woman, reducing the family, and weakening religious and parental authority and control. And it transformed art by subordinating beauty to use, and subjecting the artist, not to a favored few with inherited standards of judgment and trained tastes, but to a multitude who judged all things in terms of power and cost and size.

All this, incredible as it may seem, is in that single invention of James Watt. All this and more—Capitalism, Socialism, the Imperialism that must come when industrialized nations need foreign markets and foreign food, the wars that must come for these markets, and the revolutions that must come from these wars. Even the Great War, and the vast experiment in Russia, were corollaries of the Industrial Revolution. Seventeen-sixty-nine stands for the whole modern age.

12. 1789—THE FRENCH REVOLUTION

The French Revolution must be taken not as a single self-contained event, but as the political signature to economic and psychological facts that had accumulated for centuries. Perhaps it began in 1543, when Copernicus published his book *On the Revolutions of the Celestial Orbs;* for then began the twilight of the gods and the liberation of man. Cast here upon this petty earth, no longer the center of things but an incident, forced to realize that humanity is an interlude in biology, biology an interlude in geology (as any earthquake will remind us), and geology an interlude in astronomy, man was left to shift and think for himself. Thought became free and boundless and fought its way out of superstition and ecclesiasticism to the time when a whole age would be named after a writer, and Voltaire might say, "I have no scepter, but I have a pen."

I never cease admiring the French Enlightenment; all in all I consider it the peak of human history, greater even than Periclean Greece, or Augustan Rome, or Medicean Italy. Never had men thought so bravely, spoken so brilliantly, or lifted themselves to a greater height of culture and courtesy. "Alas!" said Louis XVI, standing in his Temple prison before the books of Voltaire and Rousseau, "these are the men that have destroyed France." Yes, they had destroyed one France, but they had liberated another, not to speak of freeing America through their disciples, Washington, Franklin, and Jefferson.

This is the best I can do, far off here in the Pacific, between two hemispheres and two ages. I look back to the Orient and wonder how a Confucian scholar or a Hindu Brahman would smile at my dates. The one would inquire courteously where the T'ang Dynasty entered into my list—an age as great in China as the Enlightenment in France. The other would ask about Akbar or Asoka, and I could only answer that Asoka belongs to Buddha, and Akbar to Mohammed.

I know how partial and provincial all lists must be. We are all born within frontiers of space and time and, struggle as we will, we never escape from our boxes. To us, civilization means Europe and America, and the Orient, which considers us barbaric, seems barbarous.

I let the reader, then, make his own lists, helping himself to what he likes in mine. Let him try to build for himself another perspective and unity that shall clarify human development for him. And let him remember the words which Napoleon bequeathed to the duke of Reichstadt at St. Helena: "May my son study history, for it is the only true psychology, and the only true philosophy."

Index

About the Author

Will Durant (1885–1981) was awarded the Pulitzer Prize (1968) and the Medal of Freedom (1977). He spent more than fifty years writing his critically acclaimed *The Story of Civilization* (the later volumes written in conjunction with his wife, Ariel) and capped off his magnificent career with *Heroes of History,* written when Durant was ninety-two. His book *The Story of Philosophy* is credited with introducing more people to the subject of philosophy than any other work. Throughout his life, Durant was passionate in his quest to bring philosophy out of the ivory towers of academia and into the lives of laypeople. A champion of human rights issues such as the brotherhood of man and social reform long before such issues were popular, Durant, through his writings, continues to entertain and educate readers the world over, inspiring millions of people to lead lives of greater perspective, understanding, and forgiveness.

About the Editor

John Little is the world's foremost authority on the life, work, and philosophy of Will Durant. Little is the only person ever authorized by the Will Durant estate to review and use the entirety of Durant's writings, personal letters, journals, and essays. He is the founder and director of The Will Durant Foundation (*www.willdurant.com*) and has lectured on philosophy in Trinity College, Dublin, and the National Museum of Film & Television (England). In addition, he writes books and magazine articles on philosophy, men's health, and conditioning, and is an award-winning documentary filmmaker.

If you share or would like more information on Will Durant's life-enhancing philosophy, or would like to obtain more writings, as well as audio and video products featuring Will Durant's lectures and interviews, we encourage you to visit the Web site at *www.willdurant.com*.